Momma, Momma, the Preacher's Comin'

By Doreen Brust Johnson

Momma, Momma, the Preacher's Comin'

Photos provided by the author
Book design by Jansina of Rivershore Books

ISBN: 978-1-63522-002-5

Printed in the United States of America
10   9   8   7   6   5   4   3   2

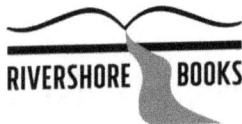

RIVERSHORE BOOKS

Rivershore Books
8982 Van Buren St. NE • Minneapolis, MN 55434
763-670-8677 • info@rivershorebooks.com

Dedication

This story is dedicated to . . .

My brother Edwin (Fritz)

Each tear I shed is of a treasured memory. We travelled a rough road together. You shall always be my confidant. I miss you so. Rest in your heavenly home as I remember you with love.

My mother Elsa (Emma)

Without your hard work, determination and sacrifices I would not be who I am today. You sacrificed so much that I might have a better life with an education. You taught me to trust in God, He would see me through. I shall be forever grateful. Rest in your heavenly home as I remember you with love.

My father Rafael (Floyd)

Dad, I have many fond memories of the years we spent together. You did not want to see your family leave. I am sure you shed many a tear as we departed from your life. I have always missed and remembered you. Rest in peace in your heavenly home as I remember you with love.

Doreen (Katrin)

*This is a picture of the cabin where the story
is centered.*

Farm Moving Day, Carrot River,
Saskatchewan 1947

My father returning home from the bush with a load
of fallen trees to be cut up for firewood. The cab is to
keep warm and had a small wood heater inside.

Katrin taking a ride in our boat (Water Trough)
during the spring thaw in our garden area. Oars of
spindly tree limbs.

Emma at age 17 returning to the farmyard with her
team from a hard day's work in the field wearing a
large brimmed hat for sun protection as well as her
brother's hand-me-down overalls.

Prologue

The wailing sound of the ambulance siren with red lights flashing gets louder and louder as it nears the entrance to the Emergency at Kilmeny Hospital. As the driver brings it to an abrupt stop, doors fly open as the Emergency staff rushes out to help. The gurney is pushed through the crowded waiting room of people waiting to see a doctor. Children are crying while parents anxiously wait for help. Someone shouts, Head injury, someone else shouts Trauma, someone else shouts get the O.R. ready. In moments they are in a room with bright lights, several doctors and numerous nurses. Intravenous is hooked up. This young patient is put on oxygen.

After five hours the exhausted doctors leave giving the nurses space to continue the care they are trained to give. I hope this young lady will wake from her coma soon says a nurse as she straightens the blankets trying to keep an encouraging smile on her concerned face. The others nod in agreement, not feeling too hopeful.

For the next three months Katrin is given the best of daily care while her family visits each day offering their love and comfort. It has been three months but they assure each other she will soon wake. Perhaps to give hope to Emma, Katrin's mother who is sixty-eight years of age? No one can bear to give up.

Several times each day and throughout the night the nurses take Katrin's temperature as well as checking her other vital signs. The intravenous drip is checked and when necessary changed. They massage her arms, legs and feet with a vanilla scented lotion. As the family sits beside her they too massage each finger with loving care in anticipation of the time she awakes from this deep sleep. Her back is gently rubbed each night with her favourite lotion as she lays on a soft sheepskin mattress, her pillow covered with a special pink satin case hand made by her mother. During each visit Dawn, her daughter, gently brushes her hair with a soft brush trimmed in gold specially chosen for it's delicate heart design. Bruce, her son, tells her endless stories of his bike and his fancy rides down the stairs at his friend's house. Still Katrin sleeps on.

I lay in bed with people coming and going day and night. They tell me my name is Katrin. Then the nurse comes in again and asks me "do you know where you are?" I cannot answer.

"You are in Kilmeny Hospital, Vancouver. How old are you?" she asks.

I hear but I cannot reply. I want to ask how I got there but they do not hear me. You just rest; the doctor will talk to you soon. Then I drift off into a dream filled sleep again.

I hear my husband's voice. Joe tells me about his day. He tells me about our home that we built together when I was just twenty-five years old. I try to smile as I remember us pounding nails and painting. He does not see my smile. He tells me my children, Bruce and Dawn come to see me every other day. Please wake up for them he says in a voice choked with emotion. I am too tired I say but he does not listen.

Again I hear voices, many different voices, some loud and some whispering. What are they saying and who are they? Why can I not open my eyes? Then I feel someone touching me, gently shaking me. The questions start again but this time the voice is different. It is stronger.

"Do you know where you are?" he asks. I try to answer, but no words will come. "We will talk later" I hear him say.

I lay with my eyes open trying to focus on the sunlight as it illuminates my room. Soon Dr. Bowie returns with his big smile.

"Do you remember me?" he asks. I answer but no one hears me. "Katrin, you have slept long enough. It is time for you to wake up. I will come back again in a few days says the doctor."

"Katrin, this is Doctor Bowie. I have come back to see you. "

"My head hurts", I whisper.

"I am not surprised," he says leaning over me to hear my weak voice. "Do you remember the accident?"

"No, was there an accident?"

"Yes, you were crossing the street on your way to work. Do you remember where you worked?"

I tried to shake my head to say no. I hear someone say that I didn't respond. They are not listening to me, I whimpered to myself.

"Does the Royal Bank sound familiar?"

After a while I say, "yes, I used paper, it was money."

"Yes, you are a teller." I try hard to think some more but I am too tired. "Perhaps this is enough for now," my doctor gently says as he pats my shoulder. "I will come back later."

Quickly I drift off into another deep sleep only this time it is more peaceful. I think of getting off the bus where I had been thinking of what I would make for supper. My family always likes meat patties in a creamy tomato sauce. We can have hot cooked sweetened rhubarb with ice cream topping for dessert. After the dishes are done we will visit with my mother. She loves to see her grandchildren. She always has some treats for them. I was wearing my favourite skirt with the pretty small flowers, my white blouse with white gloves. I was walking in the crosswalk. I feel my head. There is a rough cloth around my forehead. Did I get cut, but how? I sleep again.

Then someone wakes me. He is wearing blue clothes.

"Hello Katrin. I am Officer Judd."

He asks me questions like what do I remember. Do I remember the car? I think about that for what seems to me to be a long time.

"I tell him there was a bang and then everything went black."

"Was the light green when you crossed?" Officer Judd softly asked.

"Yes, I am sure it was, it always is. How did I get here?"

"They brought you here in the ambulance" he tells me. I try to remember.

Then I say, "There was a black car coming very fast. It was really loud, and he did not stop. He hit the green car, I saw glass and then the black came."

"Thank you Katrin," the officer softly said as he turned and quietly left my room.

I remember now but I cannot stay awake. I am 36 years old. I have a family. Where are they, why are they not here. What was my life I ask myself? I live where we have animals. Where it is quiet with only the sound of the birds chirping. But I was little then. Now I am big so how did I change? Could someone tell me? I sleep on.

I wake to find a nurse sitting beside me. As she leans over me pulling the covers a little higher she says, "Can you tell me if you heard anything while you were in your coma?" she gently asks.

"How long was I in a coma?"

"Three months" she says. "Could you hear your family talking to you?"

Again I have to think for a while. "Yes, I heard voices," I finally answer. "I talked to them but no one ever seems to hear me."

"Your mother said she had something important she had to tell you. We let her stay a long time ignoring the visitors rules. Each day she travelled for two hours by bus to come to see you. Your husband and children came too bringing fresh flowers for you to see. You have lots of pretty cards from your friends telling you how much they miss you. We are so happy you are awake," she said. She gently rubbed my arm with some pretty smelling lotion." My eyes are too heavy to stay open. I must sleep."

Chapter One

Sitting in the comfort of my modern city home looking out my window overlooking the ocean with the waves slapping the shoreline while the birds sought for food, I found myself thinking back upon the many years of life given to me. With the sun shinning in, leaving a warm glow on the soft beige carpet I felt myself drifting into a relaxed mode with memories of a life full of good times and tough times. Oh Emma, you are so fortunate to be this close to your family I said to myself.

I should be at the hospital visiting with Katrin today. Just a little rest and then I will catch the bus. While I now have grey hair due to the many years I have been given, I have also found a need for more naps. It is ok to be a little later today. My grandchildren are with her now. I must tell her the story of my life. Katrin, my dear daughter, I want you to know about me so you will understand who I am.

In 1906 my parents, Wilhelm and Alwine Scholz, left Russia to live in Canada; the land of milk and honey they had been told. Here they were sure to have a better life for themselves and their seven children that expanded to twelve during the next few short years.

My family settled on a farm near Estuary, Saskatchewan. We lived in a two-story slab unpainted house with bedrooms upstairs for the children. The ladder to go upstairs was just inside the back door. The hinged trap door in the kitchen floor also had a ladder to go down into the cellar. This is where my mother stored her canning as well as the winter potatoes and other root vegetables. Our cook stove was also used for heating with hopes that enough warmth would go upstairs to keep the bedrooms nearly warm enough.

Estuary was a village with a general store, a drug store, a pool hall, a livery stable and a postal store where telegrams could be sent and received. As we did not stay long in town, our horses were left in the field near the stable. In the summer they would munch on grass as they idled their time away waiting to be hooked up to the wagon for the return trip. In the barren season my dad would bring a feedbag to place over their heads so they could have some nourishment while they waited. As long as no one picked up the reins they would not wander away.

Two churches standing proud and tall with their magnificent white steeples glistening in the sun, could be seen from the edges of town. One church was of Christian denomination and the other Catholic, both welcoming the many people as they attended worship and fellowship services. As was the custom, the men sat on the right side while the women sat on the left both on hard wooden benches wearing their Sunday best to worship in God's House. During the summer my siblings and I ran barefoot so that is how we went to church after washing our feet at the well.

My family was one of many homesteaders in Northern Saskatchewan. As the land was not yet cleared there was a need for farmers, in the early 1900's, to clear land in payment for their farms. Your grandparents saw this as a great opportunity to build a home and a future for themselves and their family.

Finding a piece of land that was available with rich soil they began. With help from neighbouring farmers they were able to repair the house to make it habitable and warm. A barn was also needed. This they built from slabs with a sod roof just a short distance away. A corral was needed too. With some excellent craftsmanship a water trough was built from logs. For these, trees were felled, skinned and split. The other much-needed buildings were a chicken house and a pigpen. Also an outhouse, discreetly located in the brush, was equipped with an Eaton's catalogue. The catalogue served as reading material as well as toilet paper. The saying was when you get to the shiny pages its spring and so it was. The windbreak of large trees protected the farm and house area from the strong winds as it blew across the open prairies.

The building of the outhouse fell to my brothers, Klaus and Clyde. As brothers they shared no outward resemblance. Klaus was about five ten with a slight built. His brown hair and eyes always shone of mischief. Clyde was a burly six three with black curly hair and a sombre disposition. He was not big on conversation but social in a quiet way easily accepting the pranks of his brother.

As often trying to make a hard day's work fun, they got to roughhousing around while putting up the roof. Soon Clyde fell landing in the hole. This gave Klaus fuel for teasing following much laughter. Using a tree branch for extra length, Clyde was pulled out covered in dirt, but clean dirt. After Clyde insisted on how he could not use his left arm, it was decided it could be fractured. A splint was made from a slab, with a sling made from an old cloth they were soon back on the job with memories of our dad's strong lecture and no sympathy from mother. This still makes me chuckle when I think of this as I can picture Clyde at the well trying to get rid of the dirt. I know you are sleeping Katrin, but I do believe you can hear me. May my story telling give you comfort, my dear.

A well had to be dug for our much needed water. We were so fortunate to have excellent water and plenty of it. A long rope was tied to a bucket for lowering into the well to retrieve water that was always cold. Another bucket on a rope always hung in the well with cream, milk and butter staying cold as the bucket rested in the water. As some wells were known to go dry it was not to be wasted. The water for the animals as well as household use was pulled up by pail. This was a task for the younger teens.

A small one-room school with one teacher educated fifteen to twenty students to grade eight. This was a mile and a half from our farm. We always walked unless during the winter months a blizzard should be too much for us to see the road. The teachers in the small country schools were young graduates from Normal School. Normal School is equivalent to grade thirteen. These country schools in the North were usually their first school. Some had never been away from home much less in the barren country miles from town to find themselves dependent on farmers for company as well as a ride into town.

Each morning at nine a.m. the teacher would stand in front of the doorway and ring a bell which brought all the students in on the run so as not to be late. The day began with the singing of God Save the King with the students standing at attention beside their desks.

With basic classes and a lunch hour, the school day finished at four with the teacher wearing a long skirt and a fresh blouse with her hair done up in a bun would stand in the front of the classroom announcing "class dismissed". Students then stood beside their desk, as they in unison said "goodnight teacher".

German was the language spoken at home. When we started school we learned to speak English as well as read and write in English. As our parents only spoke German that continued to be the family language.

We began farming with two brown oxen, Cain and Able. While they were not known for their speed, they were known for their strength. Some years later Cain and Able were sold and two black workhorses were purchased. Eventually we had five horses to work in the fields. We also had six cows, Canadienne cattle breed, and beginning with two slowly increasing the herd, as we were able.

Each morning after being hand milked, they were turned loose to graze in the fields for the day. Since Belle seemed to be the leader of the herd, she wore a bell around her neck to assist in locating the herd much quicker at the end of the day. They were then hand milked again and tucked away safely in the barn away from the dangers of the coyotes looking for something to eat. They would be given hay, clover, alfalfa and grains depending on the time of year as to how much grass they were able to feed on during the day. They provided our large family with milk and cream, as well as enough to make butter. We also raised pigs giving enough meat to butcher for the family meat supply. The butchering of a pig was done in the yard as close to the house as possible.

I was just about to tell you about our chickens when the nurse came to check on you. They are so thoughtful and caring fixing your sheets and blankets each time, but I do wish you would wake up. Your whole family misses you so much. Now where was I? Oh yes. As I sat beside you watching you in your deep sleep, I wondered how much longer this could go on. My hopes were filled with thoughts of you hearing us as we spent our time speaking to you of our lives. Perhaps the sound of our voices will keep you from slipping too far away.

While our New Hampshire chickens laid enough eggs for our family, there was not enough extra to sell. They spent the nights in the hen house safe from the fox roaming around looking for an easy meal. Each morning they were let out to wander around the barnyard for both exercise and food, which was sprinkled, on the ground each morning. Each fall some were butchered and canned for winter meals, usually Sunday dinner.

Whenever a chicken was to be butchered I would run and hide so as to not have to watch their heads being chopped off with the axe on the butchering block. Since I was the youngest child I was able to get away with this, but it was not long until I was considered old enough to help pluck their feathers off. This had to be done just a few minutes after in order to remove the feathers easily. When I first began I would shed a bucket of tears, as I felt so bad for the poor chicken.

One Sunday dinner I was having trouble swallowing my meat. When asked what was wrong I said, "I think I can hear her clucking".

"Don't be so silly, now eat!" said Mother in her no nonsense tone.

After a time I too became used to it that they were just animals to sustain us in one-way or the other.

Chapter Two

One spring day my siblings and I were helping our dad in the field with Pooch, our tri coloured large dog, running back and forth from one to the other. This grey and black dog with small patches of orange on his stomach gave him a special look that only others noticed. Even with his poor eyesight he would suddenly see something move, usually a gopher, and take off at high speed in hopes of catching a new playmate. This particular day he was too excited to see the horse pulling the plow. He ran between the horses' large hooves but was not so lucky with his last step. His hind leg was clipped by the plow leaving a large gash. The all-purpose animal farm suave was put on with a cloth tied over to keep it clean, then tied with twine to hold it in place. After a while it became obvious that while the wound healed Pooch would not be able to regain the use of his hind leg. It was not long before he was able to run on three legs doing his favourite pastime; chasing moving creatures in the wide-open fields. He was still barking and waging his tail.

After helping in the fields during the day it would be time to do some gardening before preparing dinner. Each year our large garden displayed a variety of colourful wild flowers surrounding the vegetables. Before the fall winds blew the seeds around to replant them for next year, the poppy seeds were saved for baking buns and keuhen cake.

There was always an abundance of weeds to

pull as well as fresh vegetables to pick as they became ready for eating. A big garden was planted each year reaping enough potatoes and vegetables to feed this large family for the year. Weeding the garden was the responsibility of my mother and the older girls. Mother was a stout lady standing five feet five inches tall wearing her hair in a bun, as was the fashion for ladies. From morning until night she wore a black apron covering her plain dark coloured dress while at home.

We younger girls helped by picking the potatoes etc out of the ground and putting them into sacks to be hauled to the house and then down to the cellar where it was cold and dark. Shelling a winter's supply of peas by hand seemed to be endless. These were either then canned or stored in the root cellar. By the time I was a teenager we were able to harvest enough extra vegetables for sale.

My sister and I would take the wagon filled with as many vegetables as we could spare into town to sell, always taking Pooch with us for protection. He was blind in one eye from an accident as a puppy, but like most dogs he was eager to protect us. He did learn to not fight with the barn cats, and clearly kept his distance. We grew enough cabbage for the year to make cabbage rolls and sauerkraut. Sauerkraut was not just a treat; it was a staple to our diet just like potatoes. It would be cooked and served with the pork neck bones and spaetzle.

As there were only two boys, we girls had to work in the barn and the fields as well as inside the house. Mother seemed to be weak and sick much of the time, so cooking and baking fell to us girls. We all learned to bake bread at a young age. We learned to milk cows, muck stalls and drive horses in our teen years. By the time I was sixteen I was able to drive our team of five horses in the fields and loving each moment of it. Clyde and Klaus most often managed to wiggle out of some of the chores as they hid out in the hay loft dreaming up schemes for the next day. These schemes certainly did not involve doing work, just escaping it.

As there was no Lutheran Church in the area, our neighbours Herman and Eula Ziegler, opened their home for Sunday services to all wishing to attend which our family did. We soon found that Mr. Ziegler was a hard workingman with few words but a willing heart. Eula passed away after the birth of her seventh baby. Mr. Ziegler did his best with the older children looking after the younger ones. After receiving some gentle scolding from the ladies at church as to the presence of his children still in dirty work cloths, he placed an ad in a newspaper for a wife. Shortly thereafter he received a reply. They met in town to discuss what would lie ahead. They agreed to wed and shortly after had three more children. Unfortunately this wife too took ill and passed away. Now he was raising ten children by himself. Once again a couple members of the congregation decided to help out. They introduced him to a new lady in the community. After a few minutes of conversation, Mr. Ziegler asked her if she would marry him. The prompt answer was yes. Off they went to visit the pastor. Next stop was to his home where he called his children in.

"This is your new mother," Mr Ziegler said to them in a soft but firm voice.

After a few shy hellos Mr. Ziegler and his bride went outside leaving in the small buggy pulled by his favourite horse. They did not return for three days never telling anyone where they were going. His children did not even know if they would be coming back.

It was not long before the children fell in love with their new mother and she with them. She very firmly ran the household. Even Mr. Ziegler knew this petite lady would not let him push his weight around, which he had in abundance giving him a need to wear wide braces on his pants. Many years later it was this lady with the loving heart that cared for him during his final days. While your grandfather may have seemed to be a hard man, he was a caring man in his own way with a great love for his Lord.

It was the way in most homesteading families that the children only went to school for four years as it was expected the boys would be farmers and the girls would marry a farmer therefore no need for further education. How the time flew for me. I loved school and wanted to learn so much more. Already I knew there was a whole world out there just waiting for me to discover, but how. My last day of school was filled with endless tears.

Now it was time to work on the farm until one day I could learn more. I see you too, Katrin, have an eager desire to learn and experience so many different things in life. I have tried to give you and your brother Fritz the education I was not able to have. I always wanted a better life for the both of you.

I think it is nearing the time for your husband to arrive so I shall go home now Katrin. I have a bus to catch you know. Joe comes everyday after work still wearing his suit and tie to be with you. Maybe today you can open your eyes a little just for him. Sweet dreams my dear. I will see you to-morrow.

As I sit staring out the window on this bumpy bus at the life that is passing you by, I feel so much sadness for you Katrin. It is not like you to not fight for what you want. You have never been one to give up so easily. What is it you need to bring you back to us?

Chapter Three

The seasons came and went. In spring while the trees were budding, the crops were prepared and planted, as was the garden. The wild grass was becoming a healthy green; the thistles were sprouting up tall and silvery to show their purple blooms. The dandelions began to pop up waiting for the time to show their bright yellow heads. The deep rich red fireweed standing tall grew in abundance along the edges of the ditches. Bulrushes grew in the ditches getting ready to show off their tall thin bodies with brown fuzzy tails in the late summer. The temperature became warmer and dryer as the summer drew closer and the days grew longer. The time had now come to put away our winter boots and run barefoot until the cool fall air returns once again.

The weather seemed to be the main topic of conversation among the adults. There was always a concern of too much rain or too little. Should there be a hailstorm to break the plants, then what? They would speak at length should there would be a storm in the fall destroying the crops. Each fall there would be a couple weeks of extra warm weather referred to as Indian summer. These warm days will have followed a cold spell giving a hard frost. Would Mother Nature bring our much-needed vegetable garden to a broken mess?

The fall season was filled from sun up to sun down with harvesting in the hopes of finishing before winter arrived. The thunder and lightening storms would arrive with a loud clap followed by heavy rain. After each storm settled down my dad would go to the Field to see if there was any damage done by nature's harsh visit. Sometimes there would be a large area of grain laying on its side, which then could not be saved for harvest. The other big concern was for the vegetable garden. Canning needed to be done for our winter meals.

Then the cold winter came much too soon. The wild animals would come closer to the barn as they began to forage for food. Extra care needed to be taken so as to not encourage them to the barn or the house. The winters were filled with endless cold crisp days of snow, but also sunshine. The first few days of snowfall we would admire the soft serene outdoors enjoying each moment.

As the snow began to fall early in October covering the ground with beautiful white lacy flakes, there soon was no sight of the ground below as the flakes piled higher and higher. The sound of the wolves with their long silver fur coats howling at night with their eyes shinning in the darkness seemed so much more eerie. The quiet cold nights brought the sounds of the owls perched high in the trees hooting to each other so much closer. I liked to think they were our protectors, warning the wolves to keep their distance.

The winter months was the time of the year to catch up on mending and sewing. As we girls sat near the warm stove listening to the sparks snapping as they burnt to a bright orange glow, socks were mended. Sewing was remaking clothes to fit another member of the family. The threads were saved to be reused so as to not have to purchase as much new thread. Old sweaters were unravelled and knit into new ones with just the perfect fit.

While it seemed as though it would never happen, spring did come along with the melting of snow. This usually resulted in too much water in the ditches leaving a muddy looking mess, and sometimes in the garden area as well. Now there was the concern for the land to dry in time for seeding.

It seemed as though my school days that I loved so much were just a distant memory. I will try to give you and Fritz as much time in school as you like. May this be as easy done as said. It seems as each year goes by, jobs are more and more governed by education. I am so grateful you both were able to get your high school studies and an easier job with at least an average salary.

Chapter Four

Klaus and Clyde had been meeting a few friends at one of the farms nearby that had a dugout. One particular day after a heavy rain they felt there was enough water for them to jump in one at a time, feet first. With a lowered rope the others would pull him out. One day a friend jumped in and broke his ankle, which left him unable to crawl to the rope. Klaus jumped in helping their friend out of the water and onto the rope to be pulled up. After Klaus was too pulled up someone ran to the farm for help. When everyone was safely back at the farm, a stern talking to was given followed by strict orders to each to stay away. Dugouts are designed to trap run off water for farm use. More chores were given to use up the extra energy and time.

My sisters and I were each other's best friends. We never tired of being together. We enjoyed our time together as we did mending and other household chores. We shared thoughts and feelings as well as secrets with each other in our bedrooms. I wish you could have had a sister to share with too. I know that you are just as close with your brother, just not quit the same when it comes to secrets or is it? I know you both share so much with each other.

My brother Klaus liked to entertain a couple buddies to play card games such as poker. We lived too far out of town for him to visit the **Pool Hall** so he had his fun on the farm. The hayloft was perfect. Clyde not being as adventurous was more interested in spending quiet time with his friends.

Playing cards was strictly forbidden on Sundays, as was any form of betting any day of the week as this was gambling. He was sure our dad knew nothing of his adventures until one day Klaus received a surprise. Dad and his buddies' fathers were waiting for them to set up. As one friend was the son of the town cop, as prearranged, they were hauled into town to the police station riding in the back of the sleigh for all to see. After a severe talking to, they were given a thorough look into the jail with its' strong iron bars.

The first cell they viewed held three men that showed all the signs of too much alcohol. One man appeared to be in a very deep sleep while the other two were trying to get their attention calling come here boy, come here, in very slurred words. The last cell held two men that appeared to have been fighting. One had a large cut on his cheek while the other had a bleeding nose and cut lip.

While they each tried to not show the fear they were feeling, they listened to all the charges that could be laid due to being under age, drinking and gambling they were relieved to take the punishment handed to them by their fathers. They confessed to getting their alcohol from a source just north from someone who had access to cheap moonshine. No second chances allowed. They immediately had to mend their ways or suffer the consequences. With the extra chores handed to them, it was some time before they had enough time to meet to think up some other tomfoolery.

Somehow they had managed to get their liquor from the local bootlegger, Otis always wearing his old worn floppy hat with chewing tobacco in his mouth. Now Otis not only made and sold Corn Whiskey he had Rosco for protection.

Rosco looked like a very friendly mangy mutt with his unusual colouring of red mixed throughout his long black hair, but he had an inner ability to detect anything his master may not approve of and was only too eager to take charge. He did not like visitors approaching their small hut hidden in the trees unless they came via the main path. Any other path was permission for a loud growl, baring of his teeth, and if that was not enough a mean bark was in order. He was known to have taken many a bite out of an unlikely visitor. One loud growl and Otis would be at his window shot gun in hand with the end of the barrel resting on the windowsill. No one knew if it held buckshot or not, but no one wanted to challenge Otis. Otis and his popular refreshments were safe. No need for a 'Do Not Mess With Rosco' sign, he did his own advertising. With his good quality and low prices business was good.

Corn Whiskey is made with a large percentage of corn mash. It has a short ageing process that is usually done in barrels giving a range of 40% to 80% alcohol. Some batches had a much harsher taste than others, but it did not seem to detour the faithful customers. The making of Corn Whiskey always has been illegal as has been the selling and purchasing of it.

The Pool Hall was well known for gambling, drinking and visiting with some special women. Miss Ruby, with her long curly red hair, big smile and friendly ways was the favourite with most. With most of the men smoking, it was difficult for them to leave without any telltale signs as to where they had been. Many a man was escorted out the door for unruly behaviour. Sometimes wives had to go to the door and convince the doorman to tell their husbands it was long past time to go home. I am so glad that Mother never had to coax my dad to go home. But then he seldom went to the Pool Hall. Often children could be seen leaning against the outside wall waiting for their fathers to take them home.

Like the Beer Parlours in the Hotels, women were not allowed in until 1960 when they were permitted to enter through the Ladies and Escorts door, accompanied by an escort of course. It had been felt that if women entered the Beer Parlours they would be drawn into illicit sexual activities. Many a man was known to have spent the family money on cards and alcohol leaving nothing for food.

It was not long after a faithful Lutheran congregation was formed that it was decided there was a need for a cemetery. Mr. Ziegler was soon willing to donate a corner of his wheat field. All farmers took great pride in their fields of wheat and oats admiring their tall stalks as the wind made them wave their golden heads to visitors. This then was known as the Ziegler Cemetery. While this was not restricted to Lutherans most were. In later years, due to changes in government regulations, it could no longer be used. Wild flowers were planted to mark this special area seeding themselves with the help of the wind for the next year. Some years later my baby girl was laid there to rest. This farm is still owned and operated by the Ziegler family many generations later.

One day my sister and I noticed that a pretty young lady had started to attend Sunday services at our Lutheran Church. It came to our attention quickly that she did not live close by. Now how come this young lady would saddle her horse each Sunday morning and ride the five miles to attend our service. Clyde was taking a special interest in making her feel welcome, showing her around and being sure that she was included with the young people. Our suspicions were high.

"You seem to be very attentive," we would say.

"No, I am just being neighbourly," he would say as he left the room.

As we had noticed that several of his friends were spending a lot of time with their favourite girl, we were sure the love bug had bitten Clyde.

Whenever we had the opportunity one of us would ask, "how is Astrid?"

With flushed cheeks and eyes downward he would reply, "fine, I guess" as he walked away avoiding any further questioning.

By the next fall announcements were out that two of his friends had wedding plans for the following June. Excitement filled the community as wedding plans began. My sisters and I were sure that our family would be a part of these fun celebrations. Clyde was just keeping it a secret.

Chapter Five

By the time I was seventeen I had my eye on this quiet handsome young man from a neighbouring farm, the Ziegler's. He was a faithful member of our congregation so I was able to see him each Sunday. Not because Sunday service was held in their home, this is what he and his family had always done and he liked it that way. He was taller than my brother Klaus with a sturdy build and a shy wide smile.

He would quietly greet me with, "how is the prettiest lady in the land?"

I loved his dark brown eyes. How could my heart not leap like there was no tomorrow? Even though I felt my cheeks blush I loved to hear his soft words spoken ever so quietly just for me.

With the help of my sister and his sister who I had become friends with, we soon found ourselves being together Sunday afternoons as the rest of the young people mingled around the farm nearby after service. Because the men sat on one side and the women on the other, we were not able to sit together. His family sat together at the front while my family sat closer to the back. I could not help but notice how he would look around just before service began to give me a big smile. This made my sister Rose giggle until mother gave her a stern look which we always immediately obeyed.

It seemed most often we found ourselves wandering over to his mother's beautiful flower garden where he would pick a flower for my hair placing it in just the right spot for all to see. The fragrant smell of her wild flowers sent my senses alive and jumping. I wanted to breath in more. How I came to love his sweet attention not forgetting to tell him how handsome he was. While Floyd was one of ten children, there too were lots of chores for each to do leaving little free time for a social life. Now I had another reason to look forward to Sundays, I knew he would be there.

After a while we found we wanted to see more of each other without our siblings and friends close by, so plans were made to meet in the corn field hidden by their tall stalks to talk after chore time in the cool fall evening. To be alone with a young man with no chaperone was considered most unladylike and was sure to give the lady a bad reputation. So we tried to take extra caution so as to not be found out, or so we thought. Floyd had the utmost respect for me.

One day Anna, Floyd's sister whispered to me that she would walk into the cornfield too. She would keep a discreet distance giving us our privacy and still protecting my reputation. No wonder she was a special sister to Floyd and a dear friend to me, always caring and thoughtful.

While there was little spare time to get ready I hoped my work clothes were not too dirty. I would quick wash my feet, hands and face at the well drying my hands and face on my clothes before I hurried out to the cornfield. How I wished I could change from my hand-me-down overalls and plaid shirt into a pretty dress with flowers in a bright pink. Should I be more than a few minutes I would hear my mother calling me to remind me that I had mending to do before bedtime. Even with so many children and not feeling well, she always seemed to know what we girls were doing. Well, most of the time.

Floyd too had to wash-up at their well before walking through the fields in his work clothes, to reach our farm all the while hoping that no one would see him. His anxiety was soon lessened when Anna caught up to him telling of her plan.

"You are such a sweet sister," he said to her. No wonder everyone said she had a soft loving heart for all. Anna would patiently wait the short while to walk home with her brother that she always enjoyed spending time with. They had a special fondness for each other. Dear Anna went on to have ten children of her own loving each one as though they were the most precious gift from God.

It was not proper for couples to hold hands or kiss before they announced their wedding intentions. Then they could lightly hold hands for a quick moment or two. Other signs of affection were not permitted until marriage. Of course big smiles and googly eyes were aplenty.

When the weather became colder as fall set in, we thought the hayloft would be a better idea only to find that often another sibling had already laid claim to this warm comfy spot. With the sweet smell of hay and out of the prairie winds it was easy to see why it was a perfect meeting place. The sounds of the night owls hooting as they prepared for the night, and the horses neighing nearby added to the magic tranquility of the evening as the light sky changed to darkness as though it too was settling down for the night.

After a few months we would spend some time together after church just walking around their farmyard admiring the pretty yellow buttercups, still being sure to stay where there were others nearby. It no longer was a secret that we had to keep. By now Anna and her fellow were busy making plans of their own to wed not leaving them much extra time for chaperoning. We understood. We chaperoned each other.

Saturday evenings I took extra care to be sure my black button shoes were as polished as possible to go with my only hand-me-down black Sunday dress. After brushing my hair for several minutes I pinned the one side back with a bobby pin given to me by my mother. While I darned my stockings I knew it would not do to have a hole showing. Hats were mandatory in God's House, but since my sisters and I did not have one we each wore a triangular scarf tied under our chin while we were inside for service. These were more affordable. Oh for a piece of jewellery and a purse. What would Floyd think? Would he notice?

Two of my sisters, Floyd's sister and another friend Mary were all pairing off with their special beaus. We could not wait to meet alone to discuss our beaus, how much fun it will be when we can have them court us. Will our father's say yes, they may call on us we wondered? It would be so much fun to go for a buggy ride. Each farmer had a small light weight two-person carriage with a small seat in the back for an extra person drawn by one or two horses for when the family wagon was not needed. During the winter months a blanket was taken along to tuck around the ladies keeping the night air away.

Chapter Six

After a year I was sure Floyd was going to speak to my father for permission to court me. Just when I was sure that the next Sunday would be the day, word spread at church that Mary was gone.

When her father went to the barn early in the morning to do chores, he noticed her horse Abe was not in his stall, his bridle was missing too. Soon her beau Harry confessed that he had his suspicions that she had gone out during the night with Abe on other occasions but did not know where. Harry was too shy and respectful of the feelings of another to push. Whenever he had asked her she became very defensive so he let it rest not telling anyone as she asked.

The rest of the day and the next the men spent scouring the farmlands for miles around. There was no sign of horse tracks off into the bush, just the main road that was already well travelled with many hoof prints left behind. The nearest towns in all directions were searched. No one had seen her or her handsome brown Gelding with his white socks. Everyone for miles around was asked to be alert for missing feed or other suspicious activity. Posters were put up in each town in hopes of someone remembering something. Harry expressed his feelings that Mary had a secret that she was determined to keep. Just what it was he did not know. He only knew that his feelings for Mary were deep and strong. They had not had a disagreement.

It was a month before things seemed to settle

down, and the sombre moods began to lift. Parents seemed to relax a little more with their young people being out of sight. The question still lingered in their minds if she had been forced to leave against her will. As she had no siblings to notice anything unusual in her behaviour it was more of a mystery. I was her closest friend, but I had noticed nothing. Her parents were distraught with worry over the whereabouts of their only child they loved so much. As much as I tried to go about my life as though all was well, my heart just could not forget Mary.

Each night I lay awake thinking of our private conversations during the last months in hopes of remembering something she had said that just may give me a clue as to what was going on in her heart. Sadly, I was not able to have anything come to mind that was of consequence. To me it seemed that Mary was her usual self never complaining of her life on their farm. I wondered how could she have just disappeared with no trace. Having taken Abe with her, I feared that she had plans to be gone for some time, but where. I just could not think of any place she had spoken of.

Like all girls, we had a secret hiding place in our rooms. We did not have much to hide but we loved it. Not wanting to intrude on Mary's privacy, her mother asked me to check her room for any clues.

As I walked the mile to her house along the dusty country road, I became apprehensive just thinking of invading her privacy. She had shown me this secret place many times just as she had seen everything and mine in it. As I shared this room with three of my sisters, it was a small spot that gave me a feeling of just mine. Not having sisters, Mary created her hiding spot because she thought it was fun to have a secret that you only shared with your best friend. Our mothers said they understood and that they were sure they could trust their daughter.

As I walked along listening to the chirp of the birds in the nearby trees, I began to wonder if just maybe Mary had left me a note or a clue as to her whereabouts. My hopes began to mount. It was just so unlike her to leave by herself. Anytime she left their farm alone with Abe, it was to visit me. It was always because she had something important to tell me. This usually ended up just being a reason for us to visit together like the older girls in our community did. After leaving her farm I walked home with a heavy heart. I could not believe that she had not left even the slightest sign for me. Now I too began to fear the worst.

Floyd had asked Harry if there was anything that he really did not want to share with anyone else. His secret would be safe with him and I. Over and over again he repeated the same story, he could not think of anything. He was going to ask her father for permission to court Mary. He expressed how he wanted her to be his wife, and no one else. He had been waiting for this day for four years since the day he had gone to their farm with his father to inquire of purchasing some piglets.

When they entered the barn and his eyes fell

upon this shy pretty girl with the big brown eyes he knew he was smitten. He did not mean to stare; it was just that he could not take his eyes from Mary. She was caring for Abe with such tenderness and love that he thought there must be someone there. Her voice was so sweet and gentle. He began to dream of the day when she would be talking to him like that as they ate their dinner together.

Chapter Seven

Harvesting and canning was nearing an end, as was the dry hot weather. Soon the thunderstorms and the cold rains would be back. The cold harsh winter with it's wind and snow would soon follow. After Sunday service we young ladies would gather to discuss the times to come. We had each been given permission to be courted. Now we talked of gathering necessary items for the day we would be making ourselves a new home. We would need to ask our mothers if there were spare sugar and flour sacks for us. These we could bleach the printing away using lye soap and the scrub board with cold well water. Then lay them in the sun for Mother Nature to help us make them sparkling white. When the snow would come we would scrub them some more and then lay them on a snow bank with the sun shinning down to hopefully remove the last of the colour. From these we could make towels, hankies and our underclothes. We talked of having coloured threads to embroider fancy designs on our hankies, especially the one for the day we would be wed. For now there was much work to be done as part of the family preparing for winter.

Now Floyd and I were talking of preparing for our wedding the following June after seeding time. It was not to be even though we tried to remain optimistic. After an extra harsh winter of even colder than the usual forty below, we found ourselves needing to wait a little longer as we knew that families would have to stick together to survive these tough times. We would not make it on our own in the far north. Many young people had also postponed leaving their families to build their own future elsewhere.

The next two years passed quickly with each of us working hard to help our families save our farms. The Great Depression came hitting the farmers hard. The stock market crashed on October 29, 1929. A huge dust storm covered the prairies filling the ditches with topsoil. Soon the Great Depression became known as the 'Dirty Thirties'. The rains did not come; leaving us with a great drought. The crops and gardens desperately needed water to survive, as did the animals. Without the rains we feared of not having any crops to sell or food to eat. The wells were drying up. Many families and young men fled the dust bowl of the southern prairies to begin again in the forest areas of the north taking with them a change of clothes and a few meagre belongings. Floyd knew that when our day came we too would need to move further north into untamed land. We too would only be taking with us enough to survive on.

Mother Nature also brought other difficulties. The grasshoppers came in great numbers feasting off the barely surviving crops. Some farmers lost their entire crop to these hungry menacing insects. Wheat prices soared for those that needed to purchase but dropped for those selling. Temperatures reached 100 degrees for days on end. If this was not enough, a flu epidemic struck the region. A 19-year-old young man in the district lost his battle leaving his family devastated. My parents heard that once again there was much unrest in the world. We prayed daily that our life would be righted and there would be peace in the world once again. It was slow coming.

Oh Katrin, I am sorry to go on so about these terrible times but you must know what the world was like. I hope and pray with all my heart that neither you nor Fritz shall ever experience your world like this. We did have fun times too. Perhaps when I come back tomorrow I will tell you about my family playing Rig-marole as we sat beside the kitchen fire during the winter months. This is just a silly game, but as we listened to the fire crackling we laughed so much that for a little while our troubles were far away. Perhaps when Joe and your children come tonight you will wake up for them; even just for a minute. I so dislike leaving you like this. Good night Tochter, daughter. We all love you.

The previous few days that I visited you I was not able to continue with my story as the doctors and nurses were constantly attending to you. They are trying so hard to keep your circulation strong by frequent massaging. They do their best to care for your muscles too as we all know that one day you will come back to us. Soon Bruce will celebrate his birthday. All he has asked for is for his mother to be home again. Please try not to disappoint him.

I think I was going to tell you about one of our Rig-marole stories. My dad would begin by reminding us that we could not start with Once Upon A Time because there are no fairies in this story. Then he would say "This is how it is" and his story would begin. "I was working in the field in the far corner when I saw--" and he would point to whomever he wanted to continue. "The cutest little deer with pink spots and wearing a pretty ribbon--" Martha proudly said with a big smile. "Round her big toe and she was carrying chocolate bunnies for--" I continued. "Mother to give to us for supper tomorrow!-- " said Dad always the one to hint of a special treat after supper. "Before Martha went to the field to find Klaus. He must have run away because he has gone to visit Otis to take Roscoe for a walk to the--" said Clyde slapping Klaus on his back. "Moon to visit the man with the smiley face looking down on my silly boys--," said Mother. "Because Clyde is bathing in the tub in the yard wearing only his wool socks--" chimed in Ursula. "To find Cain and Able to bring them home to visit with mother so she can have a new hankie for church on Sunday--" stated Klaus, the family clown. "Then we can have chicken stew and dumplings for dinner and we will all be happy!" said Mabel, the shyest sibling. Sometimes the story would go on longer than other times, but we would all finish feeling a little more light hearted as we prepared for another night's sleep.

During most of the stories Clyde would add something to the effect that Klaus would need to be saved by the wild Grey Wolf dragging him by the seat of his pants off into the bushes. Then who else but Clyde would rescue him with his 'always ready for action' knife scaring away the hungry

Grey Wolf to search for his next meal somewhere else.

Perhaps it was good that we did not have the distraction of today's technology to draw us away from enjoying the simple times together. As long as we lived at home we would take part in a 'Sibling Snowball Game' during the long winter months, usually on Sunday afternoons. It was girls against the boys with both sides claiming to be the winner. Then it was time to go inside with rosy cheeks and prepare the evening meal.

Chapter Eight

One day my sister and I had gone to town to sell the few extra vegetables our family had at the Farmer's Market. Women from the nearby farms set up makeshift tables or laid blankets on the ground to display their wares. All kinds of home-grown vegetables could be purchased. Orange carrots with their bright green tops, soft yellow marrow, rich red beets with dark green tops washed and ready for cooking were among them. Home baking, especially bread baked in a wood stove was very popular filling the Market with a wonderful scent the visitors could not resist. Cinnamon buns with poppy seeds from homegrown poppies were a sure sell-out. Homemade jams and jellies were also available. For those that had the extra sugar, Saskatoon and Chokecherry jams were a favourite to sell.

Saskatoon bushes grew wild enabling farmers to pick them when they became a juicy dark blue colour. Chokecherry bushes with their tart red berries also grew wild along the side of the road. Some farmers were fortunate to have one or two chokecherry bushes growing on their farm.

One farmer sold homemade sausage, but not bologna. It seemed everyone wanted bologna. For that you had to go to the town butcher shop. Only those with means (money) were able to do so.

As we were gathering our blankets to leave for home, I noticed a horse trotting into town with a slight built rider on his back. When I was able to get a closer look I began to think it was Abe with his trademark white socks. Could the rider be Mary after all this time? Please God, let it be Mary, my lost friend. After minutes that seemed like hours she was before me with great apprehension in her eyes. When my heart slowed a little, I rushed towards her opening my arms for a hug from this much-missed friend. With tears streaming down her rosy cheeks she opened her arms to give me the hug she had longed to give. Together we hugged and cried.

I wanted to ask where she had been, how did she survive in this untamed land by herself, why did she choose to return after all this time, did her parents know she was coming home. I felt it in her hug that she just wanted to be accepted, not questioned, so I waited giving her all the time she needed to wipe away her tears.

After a long while Mary began to pour her heart out as we slowly moved to a more private area. She began by telling me that a couple years before she left she met, and in an unusual way, became friends with a Cree brave. Each spring their tribe would camp near Mary's farm for a few months.

"Oh Mary, how could you have possibly met someone from the reservation? I do not understand."

"I know Emma, it is so hard to imagine. I do not understand either why I am so comfortable with their people. I will tell you about it."

"On one trip to town, I bumped into him as I exited from the General Store dropping the paper bag of supplies I was carrying for my family. This shy young Cree brave quickly stepped forward to help gather my items. It seems he was as taken with me as I was with him and his rich dark brown eyes. With his fingers making the shape of a smile, and then on my face I knew he was saying he liked my smile. We began to watch for each other on our town trips with our families. Soon we agreed to steal ourselves a little while to meet in the trees on our farm. While we had language differences this led to a close friendship that grew. Achak, meaning Spirit, became the true friend I admired and yearned for."

"Soon Achak confided to me that their tribe would be moving on," she said.

"Will you come with me?" he pleaded.

"Being afraid of leaving the only home I knew I explained with a lump in my throat, as best I could, that I would have to say no, but I would remember him forever. To seal our friendship we each made a small cut in the end of our middle finger on our right hand and let our blood join. Friends forever."

I was so entranced with Mary's story I felt that I could hardly breathe. This could not be happening to my friend, a simple poor farm girl. She assured me over and over that it did. It sounded so exciting but I knew this was not for me. I already knew that my heart belonged to Floyd Ziegler who I was sure would one day be my husband. He was kind and gentle. He was handsome too, and he loved me. I just knew that he would one day be the one for me, and me for him. Once again Mary began her story.

"When the following spring came with Achak not returning, I began to miss him more each day. My life seemed so empty and lonely. My desire to eat, see my friends and take part in family life began to wane. I now had a very serious decision to make. Should I follow Achak whom I now felt would be the one to complete my life? Yes, I could be happy living among his people. A strange contentment came over me just thinking of it. I already loved the great outdoors admiring the many stars in the dark of night. I could hear the rustle of the leaves speaking to me as the trees gently swayed in the wind. When the night owls hooted in the quiet I felt they were bringing me messages from Achak."

Again I wondered how Mary could even think of leaving her loving home and parents to live with a people she knew nothing of. He was handsome, yes but how could she know anything of his people's ways. She could not speak Cree and they not English. Everyone knew that the Indian people were known to kill and scalp the white man. While this is hardly ever done anymore, it is still too risky. They kept to their own people being feared by the white man, and yet Mary felt a calm trust with them.

"Oh Emma, as I lay in bed that night, plans began to form in my mind as to what I must do before his tribe moved further away. I was sure that with faithful Abe we could find our way but I must act shortly. I would wait for the moon to be bright and the skies clear. I would need to see the sparkling stars for my direction just as Achak had taught me. I will find my friend."

"A week later it seemed the weather was perfect. I had been taking extra care of Abe to be sure he was in the best of health. I had been riding him long and hard each day in preparation for the trip. I was sure we were both able to handle a long day of riding. Achak had taught me to follow the sun and stars for direction. I knew we had to travel east being ever watchful for wild animals during the darkness as well as the people that may recognize us during the daylight. I had nothing to protect us but the knife that Achak had given me. Abe had a deep sense of any danger near by and a loyalty that would protect me."

"Not wanting to make me feel pressured and frighten me away, he told me he had a sure feeling in his heart that I may want to follow him sometime soon."

Mary had planned in her mind as to how she would feed herself and Abe as well as locate water. Abe would surely need both. I was not feeling so sure she really could.

Mary went on to tell me that before retiring for the night, she gave her parents a lingering kiss followed by a big hug reminding them how much she loved them. As this was something a little extra she did every once in a while, they did not become wary. The only other thing that haunted her mind was Harry. She did not wish to hurt his feelings but knew in her heart he would not become her true love, just a lifetime friend. As for me, her good friend, she knew I would immediately see through her story. It best is left unsaid.

Mary explained how that in the morning she woke at three o'clock, well before daylight. She must be gone before the rooster crowed waking her dad to do the milking. He would surely notice the empty stall. As she quickly dressed in the dark she remembered to take her warm winter shawl for the cool long nights as well as a change of clothes and an extra pair of socks should her feet get wet. She knew she had tucked her knife in her boots before going to bed. She quietly tiptoed down the stairs and into the kitchen taking with her the remaining biscuits from last night's dinner along with a few molasses cookies. She would stop at the well and fill her canteen with cold water. Closing the door as quietly as possible she ran all the way to the barn with only the light of the moon to guide her.

As Mary neared she could hear Abe's whinny. When she opened the rickety barn door he shook his head letting out another soft whinny as to say I am ready for you. With only the dawn's morning light beginning to shine a soft yellow through the open door, she quickly put on his halter and led him outside. As quietly as possible she closed the squeaking barn door hoping to not disturb the other animals should they make a disturbance.

In a few minutes she was far enough away from the farm she had always loved to steel one last look over her shoulder. She would never forget home with its little slab house settled amongst a cluster of willowy green trees protected from the prairie wind. Three mule deer were quietly nibbling on the rich green grass without being noticed. They were watching her leave giving their tails a little wiggle as if to wave good-bye. With a quick tap of each heel to Abe's side, they were off in a gallop with only the night owls talking to them.

"Oh Emma," she so gently said to me. "I really must save the remainder of my story for another time. Right now I really wish to go home to hug mom and dad. I miss them so."

I understood how she must have felt so with one more hug we parted promising to spend time together soon. How I wished to hear of the rest of her time spent with Achak. I just did not feel that it could be all that easy and fun. She was travelling into the world outside of our safe farms.

It was not long after arriving home later than usual that my mother took advantage of a quiet moment for the two of us to talk. As was her way, she did not question my sister nor did Ursula speak of my time with Mary. Knowing this would be between her and I, I shared with my mother what I had been told. After a few minutes she told me that she had always prayed for Mary that God would take good care of her. Let us continue to pray that whatever is His will is what will be done. May Mary accept this with a faithful heart? That night I was able to sleep with a less anxious heart.

My friend was safe. I wondered how long it would be before she left again; perhaps this next time will be forever.

Chapter Nine

Once again Floyd and I planned to marry the following June right after seeding. He began to repair the old unused chicken house on his parent's farm for us to live in using pieces of left over slabs and split logs. It would be small but we would still be near to help our families. Soon June 1933 came with our special day of bright blue skies, a gentle breeze, and the warm sun to shine upon us helped to fill our hearts with an excitement we could not hide. The warm fresh air was filled with the sweet smell of hay and the rich green grass mixed with the scent of wild flowers from our near-by garden.

As with my brothers, before any special event it was a trip to the barn for a hair cut for Floyd. An older sibling happily did this. Sometimes you got a good one; sometimes you hoped it would grow quickly for someone else to try. A short even cut was a good one. Then it was out to the well for a refreshing bath with his mother's homemade lye soap for his special day. With freshly washed hair, he donned his only brown suit and Sunday shirt with tie he had knotted to perfection. After receiving some loving sibling teasing his family set off to our farm. Floyd was one to be sure to be on time so as to not keep anyone waiting especially the Pastor and his new bride. He knew he was ready for this next journey in life.

In my parents yard with our families and a few close friends we shared our wedding vows before God for all to hear. Floyd was given a bible from his family. My mother gave me her thimble which I still treasure. I use it each time I sit quietly in the evening to embroider something special and reminisce.

Our brothers set up tables and benches in the yard. Chairs were carried outside for the older guests to sit in the shelter of the willow trees. Dishes of home canned chicken, homemade bread and fresh churned butter was served along with Mother's homemade dill pickles. Our sisters took care of serving this delicious lunch for all to share.

Mother had helped me make her beautiful white wedding dress to fit me as she had done for each of my sisters. Clyde polished my black button shoes until they shone like new. My long veil gently blew in the soft breeze. Mother surprised me with a new pair of white stockings. This big sacrifice was such a special gift. How I wished this special day with everyone that was dear to us would never end.

Floyd looked ever so handsome in his brown Sunday suit and tie. While he wished he had been able to stop at the local haberdashery for a new pair of shoes, he too took extra time to polish his best pair of well-worn shoes to a beautiful shine. It's amazing what a little spit for polish will do.

We soon settled into married life with both of us working along with our families to regain what had been lost of our farms. The following spring my father passed away from a tired and weary heart. Three months later my mother also passed away with a broken heart. As she would tell us how she too was tired out, perhaps too many babies, she would assure each of us of her love for us. They were laid to rest in the Ziegler Cemetery. I missed them both so much as I was just beginning this new chapter in my life.

Two years later I gave birth to our baby girl, stillborn. After laying her to rest as she slept in the Ziegler cemetery with her grandparents, we did our best to rebuild our life into a happy home even though our hearts were heavy. Another two years passed as we continued to work on the farms weathering the winter storms and the hot dry summers. Our days were long and hard but we both felt a satisfaction that the farms were going to survive. As spring came so did the realization that once again another baby was to come into our lives. We were elated. For sure this baby would be healthy.

Chapter Ten

Fall came with its' stronger winds and cooler air. The clear skies would now turn to a darker blue threatening us with strong wind and rain. It was now both harvesting and canning time, getting us up as the light orange began to rise in the far-away sky early in the morning. As Floyd was planning to spend the next few days helping my brothers in the fields, I would be helping with some canning. Suddenly Floyd burst into the house calling me to come with him. He could see smoke in the direction of the Ziegler farm.

As we pulled into the farm, we saw his family gathered by our home, which was now filled with smoke. When the smoke cleared enough to go inside, Floyd found that the old stovepipe had a hole. Although dad always cleaned the creosote from the pipes on an annual basis, he must have missed some. Creosote build-up can ignite and burn inside the chimney and stovepipes. We were always careful to remove the ashes from the tray on the bottom of the stove regularly to prevent any problems. We were so fortunate someone was near to prevent this turning into a fire, which would surely have taken our home from us. After a few days of fresh air and lots of scrubbing we were able to move back in. Everything needed a good scrubbing with our homemade lye soap.

One cold windy day during a heavy snowfall in the middle of December our baby decided he was ready to see what this world was all about.

With the help of my sisters, Fritz joined us with a healthy cry. Having given birth to twelve babies, my mother had so desperately wanted to be there to deliver her grandchildren with the love and care only a mother could give. I missed my mother so much and then with having a new family it seemed even more so. As the wind quieted down, and the heavy snowfall turned to a light fall of large white flakes falling ever so gently, with my baby in my arms I drifted off to a beautiful dream filled sleep. Please God; keep him safe and healthy in your loving arms.

During the next year Floyd and I made plans to head north in hopes of building our future in the untamed land filled with trees that would one day be our home. Our baby thrived and quickly became the love of our lives. We felt we were truly blessed. Not knowing if or when we should ever be back, we tried to be mindful of not leaving with something unsaid or undone.

There was one more place we wanted to see again before we left to fulfill our memories of home. So one mild spring day with the company of a couple of our siblings we set off with a picnic lunch to share. As I carried Fritz along the beach I told him of the times his daddy and mommy had spent floating in the salty water. I told him how I hope to one day be able to bring him back here to enjoy it as we had as he softly cooed away in my arms.

This was a very popular small natural saltwater lake was fifteen miles from our farms. It was surrounded by low rolling hills with areas of a variety of low bushy trees giving protection from the hot summer sun for the white tail deer to roam. The beach was covered in soft light coloured sand that sparkled whenever the sun shone with the salty water rippling from the soft gentle breeze. Blankets were spread out on the ground; the picnic basket set down for us to enjoy the delicious lunch as we hungrily ate taking in the beautiful serene area one last time. Even the sand flies left us alone as they sought other company.

Legend was told by the First Nations people that their people discovered the healing powers of Little Lake. Their people had been cured of small pox in the mid 1800's. Those tribesman that became afflicted with this terrible disease, and being unable to keep up with their tribe were left behind. They crawled into the nearby lake to drink and feel the cooling of the cold water on their burning itching body to lay and die. Instead they found as they lay weakened and waiting the pain began to ease, the lesions began to disappear, the redness was leaving their skin. They soon found themselves feeling their body ridding itself of this disease. Each day they became a little stronger and soon were certain they had been cured and now able to catch up with their tribe. The Cree people now believed in the miraculous powers of the lake, a gift from the Great Spirit. Word soon spread as the people came to this Little Lake for healing from assorted afflicted issues that they too became cured.

The magical buoyancy of this very salty water had been ages in the making. People loved it. They could float for hours without fear of sinking as they enjoyed the beautiful endless prairie sky. When a slight wind would come up, they would float around like a sailboat. Small Pox is caused by a virus called variola. With today's medicine this infection can now be prevented with a vaccine.

Soon it was time to pack up our things for our trip back to the farm. What sweet memories we took with us of this beautiful picturesque lake. Now it was time to see to our chores.

Chapter Eleven

I felt I needed to pay one more visit to Mary's parents. Not too long after her return home she suddenly left on the train to visit with a cousin in eastern Saskatchewan. This troubled me to think that she would leave again without another word. Her mother assured me Mary was fine and would return soon. She just needed time to adjust. It has now been several years since she returned from her time spent with Achak and still no word. I had only spent a few minutes with her by chance on one trip to town. Time was running out. I would soon be moving north with little or no hope for news for some time to come. Each time I felt a little suspicious that her mother was not sharing everything of Mary with me. Each visit I became more anxious that perhaps I should never know what happened to my friend, and why she is not returning.

Several days later Floyd's mother suggested I visit with Mary's mother one more time. I was now both anxious and excited, would this be the news I wanted to hear. The next day after the noon meal I set out on this familiar walk for Mary's house. Her mother greeted me with a big smile and a hug, but underneath was a nervousness I could not notice.

As I sat at the kitchen table while she prepared a cup of tea for each of us we talked of Floyd and I leaving for the north very soon. Then her story began.

When I was young I was not happy with always doing chores and dreamt of travelling to some fun place by myself, as I was sure I was all grown up. One day while wandering in and out of the bushes around our farm looking for wild berries to pick for my mother to can, I heard a rustling in the trees. I stopped several times to take a closer look but upon seeing nothing I decided it was just some rabbits playing. Soon a young Cree Indian about my age emerged from the bushes. He motioned for me to not be afraid. With sign languages to each other a friendship began. We soon met at the same place most everyday for the summer. We both learned a few words of each other's language. Mary's dad was already courting me with talk of wanting to marry me. I just was not sure I wanted to be a farmers' wife. I wanted something more exciting.

At the end of the hot dry summer I ran out to the thick bushes on our farm to see if my new friend was there. In a couple minutes he arrived in his quiet way just as though he had dropped in from the fluffy white clouds in the sky. As he told me his tribe was moving on the next day, both our emotions began to run high and fast. We held to each other as tight as we could as though life would now stay still. With new feelings that neither of us knew how to handle, it seemed our bodies took over. As we stood up again, Ahmik wiped my tears as he placed a gentle kiss on my cheek, turned and was gone. I remained in the quietness listening to the birds chirp for a while wondering what my life would now be like.

The change in me did not go unnoticed by either of my parents. A few months passed before

I knew I had to tell my mother what I feared had happened. One moment I was so happy but the next moment I was so afraid of the unknown to come.

After a long mother-daughter talk at the kitchen table I felt my burden was a little lighter. Mother said she would talk to my father of sending me to visit a relative until the baby was born. Just then he came in see if there was any iodine to put on a cut from a broken barbed wire fence to prevent infection, he quickly changed the subject to our serious conversation. As my father sat listening to my story I saw the worry come over his face as his shoulders slumped. He was in deep thought. Being the gentle and caring man he always was, he soon said, " Let me see what that special man of yours has to say." He then stood up, kissed my cheek and went outside.

By the next evening plans were being made for Mary's dad and I to be married. We would just have a quiet wedding. He assured me he could love my baby as much as me even if he was not the biological father. This baby would be the child of his heart. With this kind of commitment how could I have any doubt? Yes, he would be as special a man as my own father.

With Mary's sparkling blue eyes and dark black hair with its loose curls, there never seemed to be any doubt in anyone's mind as to whom she belonged. She was my daughter. We said we believed her shiny black hair and light brown skin came from my grandmother who had passed away many

years ago. As time went on we felt there was no
need to bring up the subject, and so neglected to
tell Mary of her heritage.

It seemed that whenever Mary saw a native person she became very inquisitive. It was as though
she was drawn to them, and they to her. I secretly
feared that one day she would run off to be with
her people. Each night I pray that Mary will find
her way to once again return, at least for a visit.
We both hold Mary close to our hearts all the time,
but we still think of her constantly as we miss her
so much. "I feel as though I broke my own heart,"
she said.

When she was home she told of her life with
Achak and his family. They have treated her well
so we try not to worry. Mary assured me she has
learned their ways, and feels this is the way of life
she is meant to live. While you may find this hard
to believe, she said she makes bannock each morning. I never thought she could fry anything. She
has learned how to make an open fire to cook the
fish Achak has caught. I must agree it is as though
this is the life made for her; it appears to be where
her heart is.

We were so thrilled to meet our little grand-
daughter Ashenee, meaning angel. Ashenee is
small and fine boned for her age with her father's dark shiny hair and rich dark brown eyes.
The Tribal Chief had generously allowed Mary to
teach her some English words as well as Cree. It
hurt so much to not be able to show her off to our

community. We quickly came to love this little one and were grateful for our time with the two most special girls in our lives.

While Mary was home I asked her if Achak's tribe had plans of moving on to some other area, perhaps further away. All she knew was that next year in early spring they would be heading north to live on a Reservation that was no longer being used by another tribe. Just where and how long they would stay in the north, she did not know. It would depend mainly upon the food supply. Emma, please do not speak of this to anyone other than Floyd's parents, as we wish no one else to know. You are like a second daughter to us. I am sorry I was not more forthright with you from the beginning.

His momma tells me that you and Floyd are leaving for the north too. I know this must be. There is no work here. Take these two pillow covers with you; Mary stitched them with pinks and blues just for you. When you rest your head on them each night, may they bring you sweet dreams of your loved ones here that think of you so fondly? I was afraid to tell Mary about her real father. I am sorry.

As I walked back home I had much to think of. I could not wonder if perhaps one day Achak's tribe would travel along our path. Oh how I wish I knew what God's plan was. I would watch for any sign of a Native Tribe along the way. I would ask if Mary was with them but I soon realized that she would now have a Cree name. Ashenee just may be my link to her mother. I would need to talk to Floyd about this. I just know he would willingly give me as much help as he is able.

Chapter Twelve

1938 was spent with us both working hard to help our families as we continued to prepare for our move to the north. We would end up traveling approximately 200 miles with horse and wagon before we found ourselves in the area of our new future. We needed to be as prepared as possible.

As soon as the cold winter snow melted, we loaded our wagon with essentials. The ditches will be overflowing with cold icy water. The road will be full of ruts from the winter frost. Floyd was sure to pack axle grease for the much-needed wheels on the wagon, an axe, items to repair the harness for the horses, a gun in case the need arose due to wild animals and a spare wheel. I packed our few clothes, blankets and food. We planned to stop along the roadside and spend the nights. The wagon also carried a couple chickens, a rooster and a good milking cow. Fritz would not go hungry.

For weeks to follow our wagon became our home and our barn. Bossy with her big brown eyes would be led behind the wagon for a while for some short walks as she too needed exercise, and hopefully her bathroom break. That was one area she did not always co-operate with; her timing was a little off. When milking time came and she provided, all was forgiven. Skimming the cream from the milk and a glass jar to shake it in, we were able to make a little butter for our bread.

While the dirt roads were rough from the winter snow and frost, our wagon withstood the test with the exception of the wheels. Travel was slow with Floyd having to lead the horses through some of the roughest roads left from the spring thaw. Ruts were deep. One day the front right wheel slipped into a very deep rut breaking one of the wood spokes. Floyd had to chop a large branch off a tree to use as a lever to raise the wagon. As he was lowering the wagon the supporting block of wood suddenly slipped knocking him off balance. His right arm was injured but not broken. Leaving Fritz on the floor in the wagon, I helped Floyd to do the necessary repairs. After a couple hours we were on our way before the last of the daylight could leave surrounding us in darkness. With a couple days rest he would be fine. This meant we would need to be watchful for a suitable place to stop on the side of the road for the night. I now had suddenly become the driver. Another silent prayer went up to my father for teaching me how to drive a team of horses. With Fritz tucked safely between us, we both slept very lightly that night as we waited for the light of day to come so we could travel onward.

Sometimes we would meet another wagon gently rolling along to the clip-clop of the horse's hooves, with local farmers going about their business as they gave us a friendly wave. We witnessed people working in the fields as they began preparing for the coming season, some with oxen and some with horses. We both tried to take in any ideas we could gleam from any of the farms as we passed by.

The further north we travelled the more apparent it became that the farms were poorer. Some were definitely struggling to hold on. Fields needed to be cleared of stones and roots that had surfaced over the winter before the spring plowing could begin. Here and there school children would be walking to or from school only too happy to hitch a ride on the back of our unpainted wagon leaving us with a wave and a thank-you for the ride. Most of all we noticed the vast amount of barren land just waiting for the homesteader's to come.

Our first stop along the way was to spend a couple days at a farm that appeared large enough to use help with chores in return for some much needed rest and pasture for the animals.

Mr. and Mrs. Farmer welcomed us with open arms as though we were family returning for a visit. As they had no room in the house, we would need to use the empty stall in the barn for sleeping. The sweet smell of hay gave us both comfort and a feeling of home.

We were invited to spend mealtime with them inside their small home. While they invited us to stay a few more days we felt we needed to be on our way so as to settle before the weather changed. They insisted on sending us on our way with fresh baked bread, and some home canning, some feed for the chickens and Bossy too, for which we were so grateful.

As I thought back upon our stops as we continued to travel north, I felt a great sense that all would be well for us. I thought mostly of Mr. and Mrs. Farmer and their little farmers with their generous hearts and friendly smiles. I wondered if they had felt with their name being Farmer they should be farmers. Just a silly thought. My thoughts of the little ones fussing over Fritz made me smile, as he was only too happy to enjoy the extra attention. We were so grateful to all these kind farmers along the way to make our trek possible. They too were aware of the need to head north for land.

Both Mr. and Mrs. Farmer were too happy to speak of life in the north. As they had been homesteaders for a few years they had many experiences to share with us. They both spoke honestly and straightforward of both the tough times and the rewarding times. Mr. Farmer shared with Floyd as much information as he could regard the land and caring for our animals. He told stories of when the farm equipment broke down and how to fix them when we would be miles from help with little or no supplies on hand. Floyd found this exceptionally helpful.

Mrs. Farmer passed on to me many tips of the best vegetables to grow in the north as well as a few recipes to stretch our garden supply for the year. She shared with me as many extra seeds for both vegetables and flowers as she could for my first garden. Both her and I laughed so hard when she told me of burning the dinner biscuits, scraping the black off and then frying them in lard to brown them so as to not give away her secret. You will quickly learn to improvise she promised, but do not tell. You will learn many secrets.

Most of our rest stops were among the low bushy trees for Bossy and our horses, Buck and

Misty, to graze and rest as we did as well. On one of our stops Floyd lay down on the grass for a short nap as he cuddled Fritz close, I took a much needed bathroom break a short distance away. I returned just in time to see four furry feet on the other side of the wagon near the rear wheel. My blood-curdling scream not only woke Floyd and Fritz with a start, but also sent a hungry Red Fox running franticly back into the bushes. No chicken for him that night. With my heart still racing, I began to pack up to be ready to move on. Floyd teased me that as long as I could scream like that we would be safe from the wildlife along our way.

The further north we travelled, the denser the forest became. The air was cooler even with the sun shinning down upon us like a warm blanket. We both knew there would be more danger from animals as we headed closer to their homes. We kept a keen eye for any strange movement among the trees they might give as a warning that we were too close to their home. With the sound of Bossy's bell, the horses clopping along and our talking we felt they would be keeping their distance.

Perhaps we just let our guard down one particular day as evening was drawing nigh when we heard branches breaking followed by a couple loud growls. As Floyd worked hard to keep Buck and Misty under control, I quickly reached for the gun.

Out of the thick bushes bounded an unhappy black bear with jaws wide open to show us his big teeth, and let us know he meant business. With my heart pounding so hard, my knees shaking I prepared to shoot. I knew the first chamber was always empty to prevent an accident from accidental firing, so I prepared for the second shot. In what seemed like hours nature's black furry friend turned and headed back into the forest to be with his family. As I breathed a large sigh of relief, I realized I did not know I would be so happy to see the back end of a bear.

As I was still sighing with relief, another bear came from the same thick bush. After a couple loud growls he stood up straight and tall as if to show us he was bigger and stronger than us, saying I am the boss of this forest. We slowly crept away further without a shot being fired, as if to say we are leaving your home and family safe, please do not harm us. He must have understood as he slowly turned on his huge furry feet and meandered away to be with his family. Another silent prayer was sent to heaven for my gun training.

Sometimes my thoughts went to the tough days and nights on the road where we felt deserted and more alone than we were. There were areas where the road was nothing more than a trail of rock and dirt as it seemed to take us further into the forest of tall trees with only the sound of the birds chirping and the coyotes howling in the near distance. Just when I feared that we were lost we would come to a clearing with bright blue skies and the golden sun looking down on us. What a welcome sight it was, now we were both full of smiles once again as we were able to put our fears to the side.

During the remainder of our trip the bears were at a further distance and so did not feel threatened. That was just where we liked them. Some turned and looked at us as though to tell us they knew we were there so keep going. Once in a while we could smell a fox lingering nearby or a smelly skunk in the area as they checked us out. Perhaps it was our chickens they were interested in. By now Bossy had adjusted to the bounce of the wagon with the new smells of the outdoors. Buck and Misty seemed to take it all in their daily stride as they wandered along this rough road with no complaints.

As this was still during the times when travellers would be robbed by gangsters as well as the Indians, as they were then called, we were sure to give our thanks to God each day for keeping us and our baby safe. As we had no map we mostly travelled by feeling. We felt as long as we were going north we would get there, wherever there was. The farmers along our way were happy to offer directions, usually turn when you come to an unusual type of fence or a particular cluster of trees. As we were accustomed to traveling this way we did so without fear.

As we travelled during the day Fritz played on the floor of the wagon sometimes falling over from a bump in the road. As dusk began to fall he became uneasy from the sounds of the wolves and coyotes howling. We tried to comfort him with stories of the wild dogs living in the bushes talking to each other. When he got tired of my singing 'Rock A Bye Baby|' I would switch to 'Jesus Loves Me' in hopes that by this time he would be fast asleep. Like all little ones, sometimes it worked and sometimes it didn't. My stories usually went something like this.

Living in the deep forest filled with giant sized trees were some of God's special animals and birds. Grey Wolf's cousin Silver Wolf and his sister White Wolf were going north just like us to live in the beautiful land with many trees. Their friend Hooty Owl and his family traveled with them keeping watch all through the night as they slept in the shelter of the trees. Now all the animals and people would be safe just like God said. When they arrived in Weesp they made friends with a Deer family. Now they had someone else to run and play with. Their children Elke Deer and her twin brother Ewald Deer soon became their dear friends. They would chase each other around the trees barking and bleating at each other. One day they met Harry Rabbit who was feeling very sad as he lay in the grass near a large tree. He told them how he was traveling with his family and got lost. Now he was alone. Silver Wolf and Ewald Deer asked him to be their friend and live with them. Harry Rabbit was so happy he started to hop and hop and hop until he became so tired he fell down on a soft patch of green grass and went to sleep for the whole night.

As Fritz got older my story grew and he began to ask questions. Where is Buppy, his name for all animals, today? Find Buppy and so on. His only toy was a stuffed brown bear with only one eye,

well worn from many years of play by older cousins.

Chapter Thirteen

One evening we stopped at a farm that Floyd thought looked as though they could use extra help. Just why he thought that he did not know, just a feeling. Again we asked would we be able to work for a place to stay and feed for the chickens and animals for a while as we made our way north. After looking us over for a couple moments, we were given a warm welcome.

All they had was an empty granary that we would be able to set up house in. It was very basic but out of the wind and snow. We were grateful and readily agreed. While it took us a while to adjust to living inside a building with no windows we knew we had to. We decided we would make the best of the situation using a kerosene lantern for our light whenever the door was closed. They knew someone that had an old stove not being used that Floyd was able to install. They loaned us the use of some wooden boxes for cupboards. It was not too long before a neighbour gave them a window for our home. Mr. Olson and Floyd soon had it installed. We now were a little more comfortable. We were grateful for the times we needed to be outside to do chores. We both worked for this family for a few days that turned into several years before moving on to the area where we would be beginning our own homestead.

Before another cold snowy winter with it's wind driven blizzards came we found ourselves settled on a farm in the Weesp, Saskatchewan area.

Once again a very kind farmer and his family were willing to take a chance on us.

Mr. and Mrs. Sturge was an older couple with one son Nigel. Of their three sons Nigel chose to remain on the farm to help his father break this rough land. Mrs. Sturge was a sweet quiet lady with round glasses over her sparkling eyes always wearing a large apron over her dark print dress. Mr. Sturge was a tall thin man in a plaid shirt and over-alls with a ruddy complexion from spending too much time in the outdoors with its wind and sun leaving their mark on his gentle face. Their mule Guss with his temperamental disposition, was always near taking them wherever they wished to go. Sometimes it took Nigel, a tall burly young man, a while to convince Guss that was what they were going to do, but eventually he gave in. Nigel worked hard and long each and every day showing his love for the land and his family.

While working there we became close friends with their family. They were also the only people we really got to know. Mrs. Sturge and I shared many moments together, some happy full of laughter and some sad full of tears. While she was happy for her son Nigel to have met such a lovely girl, she was filled with apprehension as to how they would all live together in their small home. Millicent was a small young lady with a feisty personality and a kind heart. Her pretty blue eyes sparkled with excitement just at the sight of Nigel. She had often made it known to Nigel that she was not prepared to share her kitchen with his mother, and that was that. What was she to do?

My favourite story shared with me was of a city couple visiting with some relatives on their farm not too far away. They travelled for several days with a 1934 black Ford Coupe before arriving at the farm. Nearing the end of the first day after travelling for some time with no break, she pleaded with her husband to stop for a much needed rest. By now she was desperate. By the time her husband had the car to a stop on the side of the road, she was out and heading for the bushes. With no time to spare, she quickly prepared to crouch down without surveying the area, but then she did not know what stinging nettles looked like anyway. She commented to her husband what pretty green soft leaves with tiny fuzzy white flowers the plants had. Trying his best to stifle a laugh, he gently explained that this was a plant to avoid. It was not long before she became very uncomfortable with no cure at hand. She now knew what he meant.

Upon their arrival at the farm she quickly shared her troubles with the farmer's wife. Like many farms there were no separate bedrooms for privacy. How do I bathe my bottom in private she whispered? Come with me, was the answer as she was led to the well. After much teasing and laughter the problem was solved. The next day was better.

After a hearty farm breakfast of eggs and homemade bread the next morning she wanted to see the animals. Off to the barnyard they went with her city visitor wearing her fancy button shoes. Who knew she did not know not to step on cow pies, and that they are not all dry. We both laughed so hard it was as though it just happened yesterday.

Much of our quiet time Floyd and I spent reminiscing of our long trip north. There were funny times, tough times and frightening times. As we had no radio and our evenings were short, we enjoyed this private time before turning the lantern off for a much-needed sleep.

While living there I once again found that I was to have another baby in the summer of 1939. Much to our delight we were blessed with another girl. This tiny baby soon showed her beautiful dark brown eyes that she had clearly inherited from her daddy who was just too happy to let everyone know. He was so proud.

After six weeks, you Katrin, became sick with whooping cough. We had no medicine and no doctor. We did our best to keep you from choking, as your little face would turn red. One day when we felt there was no hope we hugged and kissed you as we laid you on the bed with your brother totally in God's hands. After shedding more tears, our prayers were answered. While it was not instant, as we would have liked it to be, you slowly began to breath easier as the coughing subsided. It did not take too long before you were a healthy toddler trying your best to keep up with your brother. You and Fritz became an instant twosome, always together.

Bossy continued to provide milk for our family. With Red still around to not only wake us in the morning, our chickens increased a little and so did the eggs. Red certainly had a good life, which he enjoyed for many years as he strutted around showing off his beautiful colours. As long as we had flour and yeast I baked bread. When I did not have yeast we ate flat bread or biscuits. We would eat, be safe and keep fairly warm.

Chapter Fourteen

When you Katrin, were thirty days old World War 11 was declared. This was the most devastating news we could receive. Food was rationed. Coupon rationing of sugar began in July 1942, followed by other rations in order that everyone would be able to eat. Restaurants introduced meatless Tuesdays. Between 1945 and 1947 meatless Fridays were established as well. The "Canadian War Cake" grew in popularity, as it was egg less, milk less, butter less and a sugar-stretching dessert. People were building bomb shelters on their property. Others were making space in their root cellars below their homes for what they felt would be a safe place to stay.

This terrible war ended in August 1945 when the armed forces of Japan surrendered. While the war had officially ended, it was some years for life to return, as it had been both personally and throughout the country. While life cannot ever be the same, people everywhere moved on.

It was not planned that you would be born at the beginning of WW11 just because I had been born a few months before WW1 began, just a fate of life. My parents had no radio and so they too were not aware of the World happenings until someone told them after it had begun. We too had no knowledge of the extent to the unrest in the world until someone told us later that another World War had broken out. This time I was to feel it as an adult.

WW1 began on July 28th, 1914 when Austria-Hungary declared war on Serbia. This began as a small conflict that soon spread rapidly. The war ended in the late fall of 1918 with the signing of its armistice on November 11, 1918. This was said to be the bloodiest conflict in Canadian history.

As we continued to work for the Sturge family, we were ever mindful of what we would need to move on to a farm that would one day be our home. We needed to live even more frugally than ever before. Neighbours willingly stepped forward to assure us that if they had any leads they would share this information as quickly as possible passing along kind words in our favour. Some days we would feel that this would never come, then some little thing would happen to give us encouragement once again. We would then eagerly throw ourselves into our work with great anticipation of the future.

By now I had become used to looking after the home while doing my outside chores. Floyd would be up at sunrise, starting the kitchen stove to warm our home, and then go out to feed the animals before going to work in the field. While our children slept, I would dress in my only pair of work pants and shirt I had brought. Put water on the stove to heat and head out to the barn to do the milking. Mrs. Sturge would come out to help as well, but being an already older lady she tired easily. We had not only become friends but good work-mates. We helped each other. She helped me make over an old shirt from Mr. Sturge to use as a back carrier for the baby leaving Fritz to toddle along. Sometimes when I was milking I would lay the baby on the ground nearby. The best I was able to do. To carry a pail full of milk with one hand, a baby on my back and a toddler in the other hand was slow travelling but I did get my chores done. Whenever Floyd was doing a chore that he could take Fritz with him, he gladly did so.

They sold the extra milk they had after first being sure there was enough for our family too just in case Bossy was not providing enough. After checking on the children I would go to the milk house and do the separating. A separator is a fairly large bowl into which the milk is poured. When the handle is turned the machine spins and pushes the milk outward and down dividing the cream from the milk. The family consumed the milk with the remainder being used to feed the pigs and calves. From the cream butter was made. Then came the tedious job of washing the separator being sure to leave no traces of milk or cream to sour.

One day we went to look at some land to clear in anticipation of settling down but there was no building to make into a home. We needed something that was already built. We had just settled our children in the wagon when a black bear came bounding out of the trees heading straight for our wagon. Now we knew why the horses were acting strange. As Floyd tried to control the horses I knew it was up to me to protect us so I picked up the gun once again and fired. I am sure I more frightened him than hurt him as he turned and ran back into the bush away from this wild woman. I whispered another quiet thank you to my father for having taught me to use a gun. This was another reason why this did not feel like home. We were well aware that there would be wild animals willing to protect their homes from human invaders, but this many bears nearby? How would our children be safe? We both barely slept again that night as we wondered of life in this untamed land.

The quietness of the trees with only the birds chirping already reminded me of our home in Estuary. I tried not to be homesick but sometimes I just could not push that empty lonely feeling away. I knew Floyd too was missing his family. I couldn't deny that some nights I would cry myself to sleep as we wondered if we had taken on more than we could manage. We needed the help and support of our families. Perhaps it was a good thing there was no way for us to communicate with them so instead of worrying about us, they could only think of us and wonder and we them.

It was several years before Floyd and I were able to locate a farm. I cannot even begin to describe for you the joy we felt that we would now be able to have our own place to live. We would at last have our own farm. As soon as Floyd and I signed the papers it would be official. Since Floyd had never attended school he did not know how to sign his name so with the witness of a town business man Floyd, standing straight and tall in his Sunday best, signed with an X. This was his first

official business purchase, he was so proud as was
I. It seemed this exciting day had been a long time
coming.

Chapter Fifteen

It was but a few days later that we hitched our faithful black horses, Buck and Misty, to the wagon to view our new home that would mark us as 'Homesteaders'. The sight of the mass of healthy green spruce trees was beautiful and exciting, but mixed with thoughts of unending work. Next was the sight of the small one room log house that was well aged to a natural silver, nestled in closely to the silvery birch trees mixed in with the rich green ash bushes. This is where we would live and make our home.

Floyd and I were overcome with joy at its sight but nothing could compare to the excitement Fritz and you Katrin, had. You were both out of the wagon before it came to a stop peering through the window to see where you would each sleep. All there was inside was a wood and coal stove, and a round Pot Belly Heater that also burnt wood and coal. It had a screen door, rickety as it was but would keep some of the flies out. Until the paperwork was all processed we were not able to go inside, not because the door was locked, as it had no lock, but because we had been asked not to. Finally with a lot of persuasion we convinced you both to climb back into the wagon as you begged to stay longer, with our promises of returning in a few days.

While both the Sturge family and us were sad to think of parting, I was happy that we would no longer be moving along. We had found home. We would be settled before school began and another long hard winter came bringing with it the deep white snow that would threaten to bury our little log house.

We had become a family with them, one that cared for each other. We both spoke of the days to come when we would see each other again. It was like us each having an extended family in the north. God would provide for both our families, we were sure.

Fritz was now of school age so we needed to settle in before his first day. There was a one-room school a mile from our farm; he would be able to walk. Mrs. Sturge had given me two Rogers Golden Syrup pails to use as lunch pails for my children. Nigel had even punctured two holes in each and added a wire handle. They were perfect.

Before returning to the Sturge family farm we checked the remainder of the farm out. The barn with its sod roof would be large enough for our animals. It held all the signs of spiders and sparrows having built their homes within. That would need to be changed. I knew the birds would come and go, but the spiders just had to find a new home. Now Floyd wondered if the roof leaked; time will tell. The two granaries, one near the barn and the other in a nearby open field, would be large enough to hold the threshed grain for this little farm. They were both old but in good condition. The one granary was for the oats and the other for wheat.

While we did not have any pigs we did plan to get one as soon as we could. Our families had given us some money when we left to get a pig. Floyd was excited to see a pigsty in good order, ready for the arrival of little piglets. Next we checked out the chicken coop. It too was in good repair just waiting for our feathered friends to arrive, it would keep them safe from the hungry fox looking for a nighttime meal. We had been assured of good quality well water. A galvanized pail with many dents was already tied to the end of the rope hanging into the water to stay cold.

Now I thought we should climb back into our wagon for the trip back and chores already waiting for us.

"Not yet," said Floyd. "I must check on the out house, we will be sure to need that." It too was ready with the Eaton's catalogue. Now we could leave feeling all was ready for our arrival.

After doing the early evening chores we settled into our grain house, as we had come to call it, for some supper. We were all hungry. As I began to wash our dishes Nigel appeared at our door. We were invited over for coffee. Mrs. Sturge had baked a delicious Canadian War Cake for this special occasion. They were eager to hear of our new home inviting us to tell everything.

After sharing our news with them, Mr. Sturge said they too had some news for us. Would it be from our families?

"Come outside to the east side of the yard with us," he said as he led the way.

What wonderful news it was. While we were away some men from the nearby farms came over leaving whatever they could spare for us. There sat a real table and four chairs.

There was a plow and a small cultivator amongst the many other much needed items. We were overcome with their kindness. All the stories we had heard of the kind and helpful people of the north were certainly true. Later that evening we promised each other that we would do our best to help others in need along our life's path.

Over the next few days we made a couple trips to our new home to move our few belongings. We kept the chickens and Bossy for the last trip. Then it was time to say thank you and goodbye to the Sturge family. We knew we would miss this special family, but would remember them forever.

After getting settled in for a few days, Floyd went to visit a man that Mr. Sturge thought might be able to sell us a pig. Soon they settled on a sow that was expecting a small litter. She was affordable and soon settled into her new home with us. As the gestation time for a pig is 3 months, 3 weeks and 3 days Floyd needed to prepare Daisy for her curly-tailed youngsters to arrive. He did not wish to loose any piglets. This was her usual litter. An average litter is eight twice a year. When the exciting day arrived, Daisy provided us with four healthy little piglets. We felt fortunate. Fritz and Katrin were already loving their new home so these little ones added to their interest as they watched them grow from squealing little piglets to big oinkers, as they liked to call them.

Shortly after the piglets arrived, we experienced a thunderstorm. While we looked out the window at the trees blowing fiercely and the thunder roaring, I took this time to teach my children a poem my mother had taught my siblings and I when we were small.

The thunder roared,
The lightning flashed,
And all the earth was shaken.
The little pigs curled up their tails
And ran to save their bacon.

From then on each time we had thunder and lightning they would repeat this funny little rhyme over and over as they giggled and giggled. It relieved some of their fears.

While Floyd had been talking to the farmer to purchase a pig, another gentleman came along and joined in the conversation. Becoming aware that Floyd was new to the area, he asked where he came from. So our story was told of our travels to the north. Melvin, turning very serious, asked if the family we had been working for was the Surge family. At first Floyd was excited to hear of our friends but soon realized that something was wrong.

Melvin went on to explain that his friendship with Mr. Sturge had gone back for many years to when they were young lads striking out on their own, and had just returned last evening from their homestead. He was saddened to say that a sudden fierce storm had swept through that area some days earlier taking anything in its stormy path with it.

When the cloudy sky suddenly turned from grey to a deep dark black Mr. Sturge and Nigel stopped their work in the field in hopes of getting to the barn before the heavy rains and swift wind would come. The loud roar of the thunder and strong winds frightened the horses. Guss was now becoming totally out of control. The two men worked feverishly with their animals, precious time was lost. While Nigel was a strong burly young man, he was barely a match for the stubborn Guss. He could see his father tiring as he wrestled with his team praying that he would win the battle of horse and man. By the time they were able to head to the barn both men were becoming exhausted but continued to maintain control knowing there was no time for rest. That would come later.

As they neared their already shaky barn they saw where this ugly storm had already left its mark. As Nigel tended to the animals Mr. Sturge raced to the house to check on his most loved wife. When he saw the porch had been ripped from the house he feared the worst. Had she been in the house or the cellar or the garden when the heavy rain and brutal winds came?

As he reached the already crooked door that was now hanging on by one hinge he saw the destruction within. Chairs had been tossed about, dishes lay on the floor broken into pieces but no sign of the sweet lady he shared his life with. He lifted the trap door in the kitchen floor and entered the cellar hoping she would be there but to no avail.

He raced to the back yard to check the garden area. There he found her lying in a crumpled pile with her hoe beside her at the far end of the garden.

As he began to lift her into his arms she began to groan, what a wonderful sound. She is alive. Her face and arms were covered in cuts and blood and dirt but not broken. Her hair was a dirty matted mess. Her only pair of work shoes had been torn off her feet, one laying ten feet away. The garden where she toiled long and hard felt the storms wrath. With her husband's help she tried to stand but the pain in her left ankle was too much to bear. Nigel, her ever-caring son arrived in time to carry his mother into the house where she could change into dry clothes and get warm. With tender care Mr. Sturge cleaned each wound, the deeper ones with iodine to prevent infection but burning as if it were hot coals as it did its work.

With his wife now laying on their bed for some-needed rest, Mr. Sturge went in search of Nigel. Once assured that the pigs and chickens were all alive he was left to do some repairs to their homes while Nigel went to the pasture to bring in the cows. As he neared the chicken house he could hear Rudy, the rooster, talking to his flock as he paced back and forth keeping track of them all. Somehow the storm had spared the area that housed the chickens and the pigs running to the outside of their homes leaving only their water pans overturned.

The barn door had been ripped off and lay scattered across the yard. Pieces of the corral fencing had also been ripped apart. The door must be repaired and replaced before dark as to keep the coyotes and fox away as well as any other wild animals that may come in search of an easy meal. The water trough for the horses and cows had been filled with dirt and mud instead of water now needing to be emptied and cleaned, then refilled with water from the well drawn up with a bucket.

When Nigel came to the area of the pasture their cows liked to graze in, there was no sign of their herd. With these severe prairie storms not lasting more than a few minutes, but doing the damage of hours of terror, he was able to call them. Surely he would hear them or at least Bessy the youngest bawling from fright. But only the sound of the trees moving as they too tried to settle back down, and so he moved on to where he thought they might have taken refuge. After covering what seemed like the whole pasture, he heard them calling to each other. With great relief Nigel hurried to them to find that one of their much-needed herd was not there. Where could Fanny be, not just because she was their best milker, but because she too was a part of their farm family. He decided to take the rest of the herd to the barn and then return for Fanny lest the herd should bolt again.

After safely securing each of them in the barn, he readied a lantern and climbed up on Guss's strong back telling him of the job they now needed to do. Once again Guss was up for the job, ready and willing to help his buddy Nigel.

While he wanted to cover the pasture as quickly as possible Nigel knew that he needed to go slowly so as to not miss any tracks that Fanny may have left behind. Besides Guss travels on Guss speed. After crossing back and forth for what seemed like many hours he spotted some tracks leading to a small gully where the vegetation is always thin containing the surplus of water after a storm. This does not look good he thought.

Soon he found Fanny lying on her side exhausted from trying desperately to free herself from the muddy bank she had slipped into. With him and Guss working hard together they would need to move her a little further away from danger, then hurry home so as to return with the stone boat to carry her home. A stone boat is a flat wood surface on two rudders pulled by a horse usually used to carry stones and roots to an unused portion of a field. After carefully checking the sky for signs of the Black Vulchers lingering overhead, finding none he mounted and headed south.

By now Mr. Sturge was heading north with the stone boat feeling that she may have gotten turned around and headed for the gully. When he was close enough for Nigel to see him, he took off his hat waving it in large circles over his head, his sign to Nigel he was coming.

As the night sky began to lower itself they both worked with all their might along with some help from Guss to prepare Fanny for her ride home. As Nigel lit his lantern he could hear the pack of wolves and coyotes calling in the not-to-far-away dense bushes. Neither ever left a lantern without fuel in case it was needed in a hurry, now thankful for this habit.

After settling Fanny in her stall on some soft

straw to rest for a short while before milking her, Mr. Sturge went to the house to check on his wife. By now Fanny was heavy laden with a swollen udder only too anxious to be relieved of this discomfort. While Fanny has a particular way she likes to stand when being milked, today she is not being fussy. This task was a little challenging for Nigel but with patience and tender care he got the job done quickly leaving Fanny to rest for the night.

When Mr. Sturge reached the house he was surprised to see his wife in the kitchen trying to clean up the storm's mess while leaning on a chair for support looking as though she was ready to collapse any minute. She had replaced her dirty clothes with clean ones but was not able to wash, as she had no water.

Together they righted the last of the overturned furniture, swept the broken dishes off the floor and began to prepare fried eggs with bread and butter for supper. A pot of coffee was put on the wood stove to heat; everyone needed some to steady their nerves. Leaving Mrs. Sturge with warm water in the basin to wash and prepare for bed, he went back to the barn to help finish the evening chores giving thanks to God for sparing his family. Tomorrow will be a new day.

After assuring Floyd the Sturge family were well and getting on with things on the farm he was going to head home.

"In a day or so the Mrs. and I will drop by your farm to see how you are getting on" he said. "My Mrs. will want to meet your family and for sure when I tell her of your young ones."

After finishing the outdoor chores, Floyd came in for supper. I knew there was something bothering him but it would have to wait for the kinder to fall asleep. Then there would be time for adult talk.

Chapter Sixteen

With having so many chores to do it seemed we were still finding our own family routine. There was little extra time or energy in the day for anything but preparing for the long cold winter that was now just around the corner.

Floyd needed to go into the bush to fall trees to be cut and split for the winter use. With the feel of the cold fresh air and the white sky, we knew we were about to receive an abundance of cold white snow soon. The few inches we already had were just a taste of what was to come. This had to be done soon before the snow was too deep and the work too much for one man.

As soon as I had the cellar prepared with canning for the winter meals, I would spend as much time as possible chopping wood. Kindling to start the fire needed to be split too. With Fritz and Katrin's help, we would pile the wood into one large heap ready to be carried into the house. Another smaller pile of kindling was made. Soon the snow will be covering our woodpiles leaving only a sign of where the firewood lay. We will need to dig beneath the pile of frozen snow to locate the drier pieces of wood. A large chopping block, cut from a hard wood tree, sat to the edge of the pile with an axe wedged in the top ready for use. Tomorrow is the day when the coal man will come selling us chunks of this heavy black dusty rock to keep our fires burning during the long cold nights. Each afternoon before supper was prepared, both the coal bin and wood box in the house needed to be filled. This was a chore that just had to be done before dark.

I needed to check to be sure that the cloths line was cleaned, and the posts were sturdy to hold the weight of the heavy wet clothes, frozen during the winter cold, held on securely with wood pegs. In the afternoon I will bring the cloths inside standing them up to thaw leaving puddles of melted snow on the floor. Only our Sunday clothes would I iron with our two cast iron sad irons sharing one clip that fit both handles, keeping warm on the back edge of the cast iron stove.

As our stove did not have a reservoir I kept a pail on the stove with water heating for cooking and dishes. A little would be added to the well water for washing, but just enough to make it warm. I feared of wasting water the well would go dry, so caution was always in order. Saturday was bath time. The kinder were bathed first, then Floyd and then myself. Everyone's hair was filled with dust as far deep as the scalp. A thorough brushing for everyone and French braids for Katrin.

It was a Saturday afternoon when Melvin and his Mrs. pulled their team onto our farmyard. After some hasty introductions with the Mrs. insisting I call her Imogene, the men left to unhitch their team and then head to the barn for men talk. With arms full Imogene and I went into the house. This kind robust lady with her grey hair neatly tied at the back of her head in a chignon bun, wore a lovely blue dress tied at the back. I could already feel they would be the extended family we needed.

First she set a pan of poppy seed buns on the table, then the most delicious looking Canadian War Cake I had seen since we left the Sturge farm. While I am sure she knew I did not have the ingredients to bake these extras she never let on. Then she gave Fritz and Katrin a hug telling them what lovely children they were ending with 'there is a treat in my pocket somewhere for you'. Sure enough, out came two lollipops in a rich deep yummy red just waiting to be licked by small tongues. After more hugs and a big thank you, they were off to climb trees, their favourite game with their first ever lollipop.

As Imogene and I became acquainted I set a fresh pot of coffee on the stove saving the last from the pot to be heated up for supper. Soon the men came in showing the signs of having become friends too, they had much to share with each other.

As we sat at our small table sharing farm life with our new friends, the conversation turned to the Sturge family. Floyd and I both had felt grateful that they had survived the severe storm. Then they told of others who had not been so lucky.

The most heart breaking was of Millicent and her family. Her mother too, had been in the garden weeding when this sudden storm hit. Millicent had been in the barn laying fresh straw in the stalls. As soon as the heavy rain and wind eased up a little, she ran to the garden where she knew her mother had been. There she found her mother laying in the weeds and dirt in one twisted heap. Her broken body shattered Millicent's heart as she fell to the ground beside her mother. She feared she was not only broken but also dead.

When she heard a faint sound and could feel a pulse, Millicent ran into the house to get a coat to cover her. With a kiss and an assurance she would be back as quickly as she could get the men in from the field to help, she would return.

As she was leaving the farm on Barnum at a full gallop, the winds began to subside a little more. Soon she spotted the men heading toward her. After a hurried explanation, she changed horses with her dad so he could ride harder on a fresh horse leaving Millicent and her brother Charles to bring in the workhorses.

Leaving the horses in the barn they both ran to the house to find her dad was not able to move his wife, as her right side was severely broken. A branch from a nearby tree had been ripped off striking Gertrude on the back of her head, which was still bleeding. Gertrude would need a few swallows of whiskey to ease the pain before being moved. As Charles galloped off on Barnum for more help, they frantically worked together to save the life of this lady their family loved so much.

After a few days Dr. Woble said he felt that she would need constant care. Her speech would be limited and slow, her mobility limited with assistance to eat. With Charles being the only other child they had, Millicent could no longer think of leaving home to marry. Not only did Charles not have a lady in his company as yet, there likely was not to be one with the threat of having to care for his mother for the remainder of her days. Millicent was heart-broken. She loved Nigel with all her heart but knew her plans to marry and leave home were now just a dream.

Mr. and Mrs. Sturge now carry heavy hearts for both Millicent's family and Nigel. They know he will do the honourable thing and wait for her. His heart would not let him do otherwise.

Before they left for home they told us how our granary house had not withstood the storm without much damage. It seems our plan to move on had been just in time. Nigel had since repaired the door and front wall just in case another young family may come along needing shelter. Should the winter weather be kind and let us keep the roads open, we would see each other for Christmas, at their house for a noon meal. Imogene said she already had plans in her mind for our holiday visit; we could then spend time with their family.

It was hard for Floyd and I to think of planning a celebration meal knowing the Sturge family had been through this terrible ordeal. They each hold a very special place in our hearts. Surely they would find peace and move on with their lives. Nigel would not find another just to fulfill his dream of having a family of his own.

As soon as the kinder were asleep I asked Floyd what else it was he knew that had happened. He began to tell of the other farmers having lost cattle, one farmer his much need mule. Bernard had no horses or oxen to work the fields. The others assured him they would be over with their teams to help. Then he told of lightning having struck a tree at another farm burning their little slab house to the ground. All that was left standing was their cast iron stove with its tall stovepipe pointing to the sky. I could hardly believe these kind people that treated us with so much generosity had to suffer such great losses. They all believed it was a miracle that no lives were lost. The broken would be repaired. For that we gave our thanks to God

Before retiring for the night, Floyd and I agreed that the next day we would check over our buildings and fences to be sure that everything was in as good order as possible. First place we would check was the six-foot deep cellar to be sure it was suitable for a quick and safe shelter in a time of need. It would be dark, cold and a little damp but the safest place we had. The trap door in the floor and the ladder would need to be checked on a regular basis.

We now all understood how we must run to the house as quickly as possible as soon as a storm was approaching. Now we became aware of how severe the northern prairie storms can be.

Chapter Seventeen

As with every farm the mice soon tried to make themselves a cozy home near the barn with the straw piles being their favourite place. Mr. Sturge donated a couple barn cats to help with the mice task. Ginger and Snowflake were happy to do their job but wanted no part of the human connection. The rats chose the pigsty for their home even though Floyd faithfully hunted them down with his pitchfork disposing them in the far corner of the field for the wild animals to feed. Their offspring continued to come and so the circle continued.

By now we were back to the long hard days in preparation for the soon to arrive harsh winter weather with its cold winds and snowy blizzards. The Russian thistle having grown to about three feet high gives the plant a round shape. The broad prickly leaves, have now changed colour from its bluish green to a grayish brown now being dry enough to break off at the roots. This has now become tumbleweed blowing across the dry land with the winds' force scattering their seeds as they go.

I felt we were fortunate that I was able to grow a fair sized garden so we would have canned vegetables and potatoes for the coming year. When planting time arrives for the following year, the potatoes that have sprouted will be planted for the next crop. Every couple year's potatoes are planted in a different part of the garden to prevent insect problems. The plants also need to be well hilled so as to prevent exposure to light causing areas of green skin. This green flesh contains a moderately poisonous compound. These areas need to be cut away before using the remainder of the potato.

When I open a glass Mason jar I am reminded of the community ladies that so generously shared some extra jars for my canning, some came filled with their favourite tasty preserves. Their friendships will always remain with me as I think of their kind generosity.

We did expect life to be different living in the north, but little did we know what lay ahead. Sometimes that is a good thing. Leave those things to God just like we had been taught and were sure we believed. Now came the real test.

The first day of school arrived. For the first time you Katrin, and Fritz would be parted for the day. You two had become inseparable, where one went the other was. You were best friends. As I look back upon this day, I wonder how we could possibly have thought this little six-year-old boy could walk a mile to and from school alone in the wilderness. Through my tears and the trees I watched him leave our farm with his syrup pail in hand and head north to the one room school. You Katrin, would walk with him to the road, that was your boundary. All day long you Katrin would ask me every few minutes if it was time yet. So many times I would show you our Big Ben Clock and where the hands would need to be. It is taking too long, was your steady reply.

After school you would run down the road to

meet him, having counted the minutes until you would be together. Now was the time I knew I needed to trust in my Lord with all my heart. The kinner and I had been to the Little Teacher's House beside the school to meet the teacher who would be taking care of our little boy.

Miss Beulah was a pretty blond young lady just twenty years of age. She was a gentle shy teacher with a commanding presence for the unruly boys. There was sure to be some. I had no doubt that when she told me she would rule that roost, she would. Fritz was in good hands as he began to learn some independence as well as to colour, read and write. He would learn more than just farming.

I soon found that this Little School House would hold a whole new life for me. This was where the community gathered, their respite from farm duties, Beulah explained. She would also need help from the mothers that were able to travel there. Since we were only a mile away I knew she meant me. In a few short minutes I knew that I would willingly give it my all. Here lay a new friend and a learning experience I was sure to enjoy. I saw this as another opportunity to increase my reading ability and general knowledge as well as contribute to the community. I was so excited at what lay ahead.

It was not long before Fritz came home from school carrying a note for me in his syrup pail. This coming Saturday there was to be Ladies Aid meeting in the Little School House. I was excited; it was my turn to count the time on our Big Ben clock. I would now get to meet other ladies from the community but what would they talk about that could possibly include me? I would wash my dress and one for Katrin, surely she would be welcome too. I prepared the family that bath time would need to be during the morning for that one special day. Floyd just smiled and assured me we would have a nice time, Fritz would be with him.

Saturday finally came. I am not sure who was most excited, me or you Katrin. After our bath I brushed and brushed our hair until I felt it was sure to shine. I French braided your long frizzy curls so I was sure it would stay neat and tidy. You were so happy to be able to wear your only dress, a hand-me-down red plaid with a band of bright blue sewn on the bottom for the extra needed length. Your brown shoes were too short but you wanted shoes to wear and promised you would not complain even when they hurt. Oh, how I wished you had a pair of summer socks to wear so the dirt would not fill your shoes through the holes in the soles. Your knitted winter wool socks would not do, they needed to be saved for your winter boots.

I dressed in my dark blue hand-me-down dress that I felt fit me well and my black button shoes. Floyd thought it looked real nice. So I left with Katrin looking back at her brother begging to go with his sister.

When we walked into the already familiar Little School House the ladies greeted us ever so warmly quickly making me feel a part of this friendly group. I now realized that I was the only one that brought her daughter along. I did not know why, but unless someone asked me not to bring her I would continue. As they spoke of the community and school needs, I soon felt so glad I had chosen to attend for I now would have a better insight into the community of which my family and I are now a part of. As we stood with a cup of coffee, a glass of milk for you, each one assured me my family and I would be welcome in their homes any time. Should we need anything we just needed to ask. But who and how I wondered. My first task was to remember their names and which farm was theirs.

It was shortly after the Ladies Aid meeting that I received another note. The nurse from town was coming to visit the students and would need help the following Tuesday for the afternoon. Of course I would be able to help. I was excited that again I would be apart of something new.

When Tuesday came and the noon meal was finished, I washed my hands and face as well as Katrin as she would walk with me to the school. I knew she planned that she would sit with her brother in his desk, and so she did. Miss Beulah and I just prepared her desk for Miss Opal when we heard her pull into the yard with her horse and buggy. One of the older boys was sent out to tether her horse to the hitching post leaving him enough water and hay for her visit.

After Miss Opal was introduced to the students she explained that first of all she would check the eyesight of each student. Now I knew for sure that this was a benefit we would not be able to provide for our children. Then she went through her list of students that were due to receive an inoculation.

Inoculations for the prevention of polio were introduced in the mid 1940s. Prevention for diphtheria, pertussis (whooping cough) and smallpox was also introduced during the 1940s. A careful record was kept by the nurse for each school district administering to students as needed.

At the end of the afternoon I thanked Miss Beulah for letting me help and assuring her I would be willing to assist another time. This was an opportunity for me to meet the children in the community that my children were associating with.

Chapter Eighteen

By now Fritz had settled into school of approximately twenty students each year, making his special friends. Classes were for students from grade one to grade seven. He talked frequently of two boys in particular. As you Katrin, went to meet him after school you both came running into the yard crying your heart out this one-day.

Before class was dismissed Miss Beulah explained to the class that Clay had not come to school that day, as there had been an accident on their farm the evening before. While helping with the barn chores, something spooked one of their horses causing him to step backwards so as to get away from what he felt was danger. In doing so he kicked Clay knocking him over and then stepping on his foot crushing it instantly. His hoof hit Clay on the side of his head looking as though it had caved in his temple.

Clay's parents tried their best to stop the bleeding and the pain their youngest son was having. Clay's older brother quickly mounted the nearest horse that was still bridled and headed from the farm in a full gallop. He knew he needed to travel the eight miles as quickly as possible to get help for his little brother. Annoying as little brothers can be sometimes, he loved him with his whole heart. The only doctor just had to be in town.

As Jack galloped past a farmer's barn, the visiting Veterinary knew there was something very wrong. The two men mounted and headed to the

Baker farm fearing the worst had happened. Being a small country town there was no trained animal doctor, just someone with a heap of practical experience that the farmers called their Horse Doctor.

Upon arrival at the farm, Leroy checked Clay's head to asses the injuries. After washing most of the blood away, he was sure it was not a deep injury, more of a graze scraping his cheekbone and temple. In time it would heel leaving a few scars behind as evidence, but for now poor Clay would have much pain to endure. Leroy was adamant that Clay not be moved before Doc. Brown examined him. This would be a while yet.

As they tried to hold Clay still he became more agitated and frightened. A sip of whiskey would just maybe work. His boot needed to be removed as his leg began to swell. Leroy knew the most important thing was to save his foot, but to cut off his only boot was not what he wanted to do. As the laces were made from twine he decided he would cut through what he felt was the most practical way. Working quickly before the foot had swollen too much; he pulled the twine away as to open the top of the boot as much as possible. With the help of Clay's father they removed the boot with Clay's screams echoing through everyone's minds. I am so sorry young lad was all Leroy could utter.

Several hours later Doc. Brown finished with a thorough examination and began preparations to take Clay to the town hospital, an eight-mile ride in his buggy over the rough roads. Zoro would know when to pull at a slow even trot as to make his young patients' ride as comfortable as possible. Zoro was a small American Quarter horse having a black mane and tail giving his light brown colouring a regal look with his head held high. Mrs. Baker would sit with her son to both comfort and keep him awake.

Once at the hospital, a call would be made to Doc. Murphy in Cross Cut thirty miles away with hopes of him arriving tomorrow in his small bright orange aircraft. Perhaps together they could save his foot and ease his pain. First, they must make a stretcher to move him to the buggy and then the ride to town.

Once there Doc. Brown decided it best to let him spend the night on the operating table to save having to move him again which would just add to his pain. With makeshift sides and a little chloroform, and much comfort from his parents Clay drifted off to a quiet sleep.

Doc. Murphy would leave in the morning as soon as the darkness left giving new light to the day to see his way. With the sun peeking out Doc. Murphy hurried to the hospital carrying his large black medical saddlebag. He would need much of his essential equipment as he could carry and perhaps more. The last item to be placed inside was his favourite harmonica. He could be heard approaching by the sound of Me and the Man in the Moon played in perfect tune.

Entering this small white immaculate hospital he was greeted by a nurse, but with only time for a polite nod in return he hurriedly entered the operating room where his new young patient lay moaning with pain. This was never something a doctor wanted to see. Trying to sound as reassuring as possible for both Clay and his parents he calmly spoke of fixing up that bum leg.

Even with cold cloths covering his leg and forehead throughout the night things did not look good. First he would check his head to be sure it was just a graze and not a fractured skull. With having no technical equipment available he felt confident that the head wound would not be life threatening. Later they would be able to tell more, he knew his name and where he was. This was a good sign.

Following a lengthy but careful examination of the foot, the worst he had feared would come to follow. The young lad's foot would need to be amputated. That meant a trip to Cross Cut with only one family member along for the ride and to give comfort. The best he could do now was to pray that he would not loose more than his ankle and foot but he must hurry before gangrene can even think of setting in. Taking extra care to not alarm anyone he must speak privately with the parents to have their understanding and consent.

With a tearful heart Mr. Baker decided it best that Mrs. Baker accompany their son. He had the farm work to do. The neighbours would feed this man that could not cook. How he wished he had tried to help inside the house. That will change, he promised himself but for now we will do the best we can.

Throughout our close-knit community anxiety grew. There was no way for Mr. Baker to receive word as to Clay's situation for at least a few days. Then he would need to make a trip to town in hopes of a telegraph, Morse code made up of dots and dashes, waiting for him. Should another neighbouring farmer have needed to go to town, they would inquire as to there being a message. Either way a trip to the Baker farm would be taken as soon as possible in an attempt to help ease the worry. A loaf of homemade bread usually accompanied the messenger.

Five long days later word arrived that Clay's foot and ankle had been amputated. It would be some time before this young lad would be released from hospital. A very kind older couple in Cross Cut had taken Mrs. Baker in to live with them to be near her son as he began his lengthy recovery. Being within walking distance, Mrs. Baker spent the days and evenings with Clay taking her meals with her as she assured him he was a strong young lad with a full life ahead. Together with his family at his side, he would make it.

Some weeks later Doc. Murphy said he needed to make the trip to their hometown to remove tonsils from another young patient. Mrs. Baker and Clay could ride back with him.

Weary with stress and the unknown they said their goodbyes to the kind and caring couple that had shared their home and hearts with them. A pair of crutches had been hand made from a Birch tree with the bottom portion covered with leather

donated by the local cobbler. Clay had made progress each day giving him the assurance that his life
would get better too.

When Miss Beulah heard this good news she
began to prepare the students for the return of
their friend. They would make changes to their
noon hour and recess games to include Clay. Sometimes a referee was needed. The students quickly
began to talk of ways to make their friend feel part
of the class.

By the time Clay was able to return to school,
a neighbour said he had a gentle Black Friesian
Horse in his pasture that was too old to work. Mr.
Baker was too happy to purchase him for a very
small fee; he would pull a small wagon or sleigh for
a few years to come. Clay would now have his independence. With Clay's gentle care he and Midnight
would soon be a team.

By the time Clay was ready to return to his
studies, an added stall was built on the horse shed
to accommodate Midnight and the wagon/sleigh
he would bring his new master in. Each day Clay
would bring lunch of hay and water for Midnight
as well as his own. Before leaving for home Clay
would faithfully muck his stall readying it for the
next day. With the help of a couple friends he too
would soon be on his way home leaving with a feeling that each and every day was a little easier.

By now the fall wind was having a real bite to it
giving that feeling of the winter storms that were
hiding just around the corner. Having enjoyed a
few weeks of Indian summer, we just did not feel

ready to have the warm afternoon sun leave us just yet. We knew the seasons in the north were distinctive as they came and went; now it was time for winter to visit. It was time to prepare for the cold outdoors with handmade wool socks for our boots, winter parkas and mitts. Rumour was the Indians were predicting more blizzards and deeper snow than had been seen for many moons.

For sure the fence posts holding up our rail fence would be covered with nature's white sparkly snow no longer leaving a marker for the road edge hiding the deep ditches. I must ask Floyd to be sure to have a stick from a tree branch cleaned of its smaller limbs ready for Fritz to use to check the snow depth before stepping lest he fall into a soft spot and not be able to get out. Miss Beulah will check each student for frostbite as they enter the Little School House. Those students will need to sit further away from the heater for a while giving time for their bodies to slowly warm. For now I must hurry to finish the last of the fall canning. I would also need to carefully check each wall for signs of light coming through. These spots would need to have a covering of clay both inside and outside to be sure they were well sealed keeping the cold and wind out. We could not afford to lose any precious heat from our little log home.

As Floyd began to prepare to change our wagon into our winter sleigh snow flurries began to fall. By the next day the ground was covered past his ankles with clean sparkly white flakes telling us they were here to stay. Once again it was time for him to hurry before the snow fell too deep to head north into the bush with his buck saw to bring home our winter's supply of logs cleaned and ready to be cut into stove length firewood. It would then need to be split and piled as soon as possible. With the sun's reflection from the white snow it seemed the days were a little longer giving us the extra needed light for these added chores.

Again Fritz came home with a note from Miss Beulah, it was time for the Farmer's Fall Social to be held on Saturday evening at eight o'clock in the Little School House. After tying our team to a rail in the barn shelter, we entered to find the desks had been moved to the outsides of the room for the children to sleep on, but first they would hold their parents coats. Being so warmly greeted we felt that we had attended many times before.

Soon Martha began to play the poorly tuned piano with several men chiming in on their mouth organs, guitars, spoons and anything else they had to play leaving the rest to dance on the freshly waxed floor. Later in the evening someone would sprinkle more wax as though they were spreading feed for their chickens with their fingers.

Soon Floyd and I decided it would be the time for us to join in the merriment. As we stepped onto the dance floor, I noticed out of the corner of my eye, you Katrin and Fritz were having a great time with your friends you had already made. Now I knew we would all fit in, life would be good.

As the evening wore on and the children became sleepy, parents made them comfortable on a couple desks moved together covering each with a coat after a quick trip in the dark to the outhouse. Not having taken part in much dancing before we soon were able to dance the two-step and polka with the help of our new friends so willing to teach us both. What a great time we had, laughing and dancing the evening away.

The middle of the night came along with the cleaning and rearranging of the Little School House in preparation of Monday classes. When all was finished coats were put on the sleeping children while horses were hitched to the family sleigh. Children were carried out in the minus forty-degree weather for the ride home. As you huddled together I covered you both with a blanket to keep you warm. Soon we would be home out of the brisk cold night air tucking you into your beds, which had by now cooled down. Floyd would check on the other animals while he was in the barn settling Buck and Misty with their now white frosty faces down for the night. Tomorrow he would brush their long furry coats and check each hoof to be sure there was nothing there to give them discomfort. We were so dependent on these two hard working beautiful horses.

This Social was the evening for the farmers to check on each of their neighbours willingly offering any help they could give. We were happy to learn that Clay was making steady improvement. His leg had healed nicely but he clearly was in need of bigger crutches as he continued to grow. Miss Beulah said he was back to his former self, laughing and playing with the other students. All students were treating him with respect but not pampering him as he became more independent with all the signs of developing into a healthy and happy young man.

Chapter Nineteen

As for the other neighbours, all had been well with only one worrisome incident that ended well. We learned that one family had two daughters in their early teen years. The older daughter was known to sleep walk. As they both slept in their hayloft that was connected to the side of their house, she could not be heard leaving during the night as her sister slept soundly nearby.

It was when the weather was showing its sign of winter to come but not leaving its winter snow to cover the ground that Alice made her way into the dark. When her sister Margaret woke to find her gone, she quickly woke their parents. With lantern in hand, their father set out on horseback in hopes of finding Alice still on their farm repeatedly calling her name. Until now Alice had only walked to the barn to lie in the stall with her favourite horse but not this night. With no immediate means of enlisting the help of the neighbours, they did the best they could with only the light of the moon and one small lantern.

As they each tried to think of a positive outcome their minds went to all the possible dangers Alice could be in. Had she fallen and seriously hurt herself leaving her not able to take shelter? Had a wolf or a coyote found her? Was she dreaming of fetching water from the well and had fallen in?

As their hearts raced they willed an early morning light to rise. They continued to search as best they could, each knowing they would have to wait a little longer. The dark sky would not give way to the light of day for a while yet.

As Mr. Burns turned his mount around to return to the farm to wait for daylight he thought he heard the sound of another traveller on the road in the still night. He felt the nervousness in his horse as he too wondered who would be out in this black cold night. As he wondered if someone had found Alice and was about to keep her or worse yet, do her harm, his stomach began to churn. This could not happen to his little daughter that was so sweet and loving to all. Worse yet, he hoped and prayed that she had not fallen prey to an angry wolf or coyote, and had been dragged into the bush.

He decided to go towards the wagon sounds travelling as safely as he could lest his horse was to stumble in a rut. In what seemed liked hours he met the wagon carrying his neighbour and family on their way home from visiting with friends.

The Gibbs explained how their horses had turned a corner too sharp with the wagon going over the edge of the road and sliding into the slope of the ditch. With working in the dark by them, it had taken an extra hour before they were back on their way. This explained why they were travelling so late into the night.

The most disappointing news was that they had not heard or seen anything unusual. Plans were made to begin a search. The light would come in a short while now. While they waited for more light they searched the farm once again to no avail. It was decided that Mr. Burns would travel north alerting other neighbours along the way. Just maybe she was dreaming of going to school. She always missed her school friends.

After returning from taking his family home, Mr. Gibbs took the south road leading to town. He would also alert the farmers along his way knowing they too would be joining the search. They must all have faith that soon Alice would be found.

As Mr. Gibbs travelled nearing two miles calling her name, his horse suddenly stopped on the road. Refusing to go any further his fears began to mount. After calling her name louder and louder for a short while, he heard a menacing growl from the edge of the bushes that sounded only too familiar. This called for a warning shot into the air as well as to alert the other searchers he may be onto something. After a few minutes he would send another warning high into the air before dismounting to take a closer look at what he feared the most. If Alice was still alive would she wake up and be old enough to know that the second shot meant help was there.

Soon with heart pounding so loud he could not hear himself breath, he knew it was now time to take a closer look. Leaving his horse on the side of the road he jumped the deep snowy ditch to get closer to the bush, he could hear the sound of another shot fired into the air in response. He again began to call to Alice for reassurance that it was her dad's friend coming to help and perhaps frightening the wolf away.

It was several minutes after arriving at the

edge of the bushes that he began to hear a faint cry. Begging Alice to be brave and call out to him so he could reach her, he heard her reply, "I am here up in the tree. Please help me."

What a welcome sight it was. High up in a poplar tree hanging on for dear life, was Alice. She had been so frightened that she had climbed as high as she could fear the wolf would reach her. Now to get this frightened girl to come back down. Mr. Gibbs just could not climb due to health and age. She would need to trust with all her heart and do as asked.

Step by step, branch-by-branch Alice began to inch her way lower and lower. Her tears had now stopped. She could do it.

By the time Alice was low enough to drop into the arms of Mr. Gibbs, her father had arrived to witness this beautiful sight. Now it was daddy's turn to shed the many tears of joy and relief.

After Alice was safely home sitting at the table with her family warming up with a cup of hot cocoa, she began to tell of waking up on the road as her mother cleaned the cuts on her hands. Hearing the sound of wolves getting nearer, she decided it best to locate a tree she could climb in hopes of being out of their angry reach. Then she told of the two grey wolves pacing around the tree with jaws wide open, snapping their teeth at her. She decided not to move, just hang on and wait. They too sat in wait at the bottom of the tree.

It was the sound of gunshot that sent them running further into the bush. Not knowing how far they had gone Alice made the wise decision to just stay put until daylight in hopes of someone going by that could help her.

Mr. Burns was already thinking of ways to protect his family from such an incident again. He would also speak with Mr. Jackson as they too had a son that walked in his sleep.

As I split wood one afternoon in preparation for our winter supply, I found myself thinking back over the harsh times our neighbours and we must endure. I also thought of the beautiful hot summer days filled with bright sunshine beating down on us as we worked in the fields. How we wished for a little breeze to keep us cool with having so little time to rest in the shade. Everything was dry and dusty needing a drink of fresh rain, but just a little light rain.

By late August the beautiful delicate butterflies began to fly south leaving behind a sign that winter is nearing. By October the robins with their bright red breasts have added down feathers for their insulation for the coming winter. Slowly they also began to migrate south in search of food. As we watch our feathered friends leave we feel a kind of sadness that the harsh winter is soon upon us.

Chapter Twenty

As had been predicted by the Chief of the local Indian tribe this winter was showing all the signs of being extra harsh. The snow was already up to my chest with drifts much higher. The winds were stronger giving the air a much colder feel than the estimated temperature of now minus forty-five degrees. With no thermometer or radio to tell us, we had to wait for word from someone else as to the radio report. The wind would howl all through the night keeping the coyotes company as they called to each other.

By morning the snow had piled itself half way up the door leaving Floyd the task of digging his way out. Somehow he had to make his way to the barn. There he then had to clear the deep crisp snow from the door. The wind was only too happy to either help him open the door or close it depending upon Nature's chosen direction for that day. The northern winds do earn their reputation blowing one way and then the next, sometimes all in the same day. When the front barn door was snowed in, so was the back door that led to the handy straw stack.

Floyd's next big job was to feed and water all the animals pulling the water from the deep dark well with a bucket. Before completing the remainder of the chores he would make his way back to the house for a cup of hot coffee and some breakfast, a time to warm up as well.

When Floyd would leave the house in the morning I would lay for a couple minutes under our grey army blankets convincing myself that I too must get up into the cold house to prepare our breakfast before beginning the daily chores. Some mornings it was a struggle.

After dressing and making the bed I would move a big pot of water to the hottest part of the stove to heat for washing our hands and faces. Then the aluminium coffee pot that I had left filled with water before going to bed would need to be moved to the hotter part of our cast iron stove. Stir the fire in the cook stove, which was now beginning to crackle and add more wood. By now I had a big pot of slow cooking oatmeal porridge cooking to fill everyone's hungry tummies for the morning.

Soon it was time to wake my kinner before leaving for the barn to do the milking. The cows would be eagerly waiting for me with their udders heavy with milk. They would make their beds, and then stand in front of the open oven door to dress. Here they could feel some warmth as they stood shivering in their underclothes. Katrin would stand on the oven door and stir the porridge for me always hoping it had not stuck to the bottom of the pot too much. They then had a few minutes to giggle and fool around with the dog before Floyd and I came in carrying a bucket of fresh milk and the separator. While they ate their breakfast I finished separating the milk leaving the separator and the porridge pot for them to wash before going to school. Their treat was to have a little cream on top of their porridge making the already whole milk a little richer. There was no sugar for them so we felt they deserved this treat.

As long as the snow was not blowing too much for them to see, I insisted they go to school. I so wanted them to get an education for a better life. First Floyd would need to break a path from the house to the road with one of the horses. Each snowy morning he would try to convince me that our kinner should not go to school until the weather improved, this could be spring. I stuck to my rule that if at all possible they would not stay home. I would help them fight the bitter north to grow up strong and educated telling them how nothing came easy.

While they put on their boots, parkas and mitts I made their lunch of homemade bread and butter. Some days it was just plain bread. Sometimes I would have some Roger's Corn Syrup to spread between the slices when the bread was becoming a little stale. They enjoyed it as by the time they reached school their sandwiches were frozen giving a crisp crunchy treat. What they enjoyed the most was griebenschmalz on their bread in place of butter. That too I had to limit.

Griebenschmalz was made on butchering day. Once a year most farmers would butcher one of their pigs along with the help of neighbours. After the meat was hung in their yard near the house, then cut up, some of the rind was cleaned and placed in a pan in the oven to brown until crispy. After cooling to a lukewarm stage it was put through the meat grinder along with some of the lard, salt and pepper. This would then be about the consistency of peanut butter. Jars were then filled; lids put on to seal, and carried down to the cellar to wait for the day when a special treat was needed.

I always felt it would have been nice to have made a larger quantity as we had plenty of rind but the lard was needed for cooking as well as to make our years supply of soap for both personal and laundry use. Every home had a washstand next to the slop pail. On it sat a enamel basin with cold water and a bar of soap resting on a chipped saucer I had found. To make soap, lard was mixed with a portion of lye until it was smooth. I would shape it into squares and set it outside to dry in the air. Then it was stored in the cellar. This soap was good for washing the laundry on the scrub board. Lard soap is a good cleanser and gentle on your skin leaving it soft and moist.

As the snow piles higher and higher, the drifts become deeper and harder now frozen from the cold, I start to have thoughts of us leaving this frozen north and going a little further south closer to a town where the kinder will have some chance of an education giving them a better future. After speaking with other neighbours I begin to feel that life will always be just a meagre existence. I now know I must think of this long and hard keeping my thoughts and fears to myself lest I frighten Fritz and Katrin.

Harvesting season was now finished, as was the canning. Floyd would once again hitch the team to the sleigh and head further north for the day to fell trees for our winter's firewood. There he would meet with other men from the community also in need of firewood.

The time had come when we could visit with Melvin and Imogene. We all had been anticipating this wonderful day for weeks. Would Mother Nature descend upon us with her wrath or would she be kind to give us a few days of her best weather. I could not take my eyes from the window where I watched the sky constantly with great apprehension as I worked. I missed not seeing the cows grazing around the backyard, as they would slowly find their way to greener pastures. There they would often find shelter in the midst of the green willows, some to just lay and rest on the soft green grass as they chewed their cuds.

The day before our visit began with bright blue skies that seemed to go further than the eye could see. There were just a few fluffy white clouds softly floating around in various shapes waiting to be admired. The morning sun came up shinning a beautiful gold to light our day as it reflected off the pristine sparkly snow. Already the day felt warmer and happier, my heart was lighter, and there was hope for another nice day.

The day was spent with each of us doing our chores a little quicker and cheerier. Extra wood needed to be split and carried inside filling the wood box until one more stick would collapse the pile. Extra coal needed to be brought in until the coal bin was heaped as high as it could go without spilling its' dirty black dust everywhere. Fritz and

Katrin helped in the barn spreading clean straw for the animals where Floyd had mucked. Next they cleaned the chicken pens leaving behind soft beds and fresh water. The horses were brushed a little longer this day. I baked bread as I had come to know that a loaf of fresh baked golden brown bread was always a welcome and needed gift for any family. It was a caring and friendly gesture.

By the time Floyd and I were ready for bed we were both exhausted and excited. Visiting with these special people that had become our dear friends was much needed to help fill the home-sick feeling we were both having again. I must ask Imogine if she knew of an Indian Tribe in the area. Floyd said he would try to remember to speak to Melvin as well.

The following morning we woke to the sound of Big Red crowing in the barnyard. We all jumped to our feet before our eyes were open eager to get a start on this exciting day. No one complained of the cold house or that some water had been left in the washbasin and was now frozen. Winter was here. Jack Frost had coated the inside of the windows with his special designs for us all to admire. The kinner would scrape their fingernails in the designs.

Soon we were ready to put our things into the sleigh to make this much-awaited trip. Buck and Misty showed their excitement too as they could not stand still. As we pulled onto the road there was the beautiful sight of three mule deer meandering along the bush line. Were they too going to visit their friends?

Nearly two hours later we pulled onto the farmyard of our friends who were already eagerly waiting for us. We had only met one sleigh travelling at a steady pace giving us a friendly wave as we passed. I was so happy to see Imogene that I was overtaken with emotion. She was not my sister that I had left behind, but was a dear sweet friend. We always had much to talk of as had Melvin and Floyd. They were like family to us.

As soon as warm greetings had been shared, and our horses taken to the barn, we were all sitting around their large wood table covered with a bright orange table cloth, enjoying the taste of fresh baked cinnamon buns and hot coffee as we warmed ourselves from the cold outdoors. I can still see Fritz and Katrin enjoying their second bun with huge grins. At home I could only give them one each.

Now that their tummies were filled, they quickly put on their boots and parkas to head to the barnyard. First they would gather any eggs there may be for Imogene. The biggest attraction was to say hello to Sandy, their light brown pony with his long tail nearly touching the ground. Later they would each have many rides, enough to talk of for days to come.

As soon as they left the house Pepper was there to greet them. Pepper was a large grey and black dog that had been found wandering alone in town. When no one knew where his home was, Melvin said he felt Pepper would get along just fine with

Max, another black stray they had rescued a few years earlier. Even though Max was accustomed to ruling his territory, he readily took Pepper in. As long as Pepper did not overstep his boundary they got along well.

Some months later Max rushed to the aid of one of their cows grazing in the pasture. A coyote had come too close. As hard as he tried to frighten this coyote away, this hungry beast stood his ground. Max gave his life to save this cow that was a part of their animal family. It was Pepper that sent the coyote running.

For weeks Pepper was lethargic with no desire to eat or drink. With an extra amount of attention he began to perk up each time he saw Sandy. He chose to spend the night sleeping beside Sandy in his stall. They were now best friends. An orange barn cat was often seen tolerating Pepper. As her only job and interest was to catch mice, she never showed any friendship to Max, but somehow Pepper was different. Melvin never encouraged this bonding, for some reason Sandy did.

When Melvin and Floyd went to the barn, Sandy was haltered and led into the corral for Fritz and Katrin to ride, fairly patiently taking turns. As Sandy was now to old to run, he gently walked around and around in his always steady pace.

As the men stood observing from the sidelines Floyd said he brought up the subject of an Indian Tribe living in the area during the past season. Melvin said there was one but had moved on a couple weeks earlier. He had heard from another farmer in town that they were expected back in spring. Just where they would be spending the winter he did not know, nor had he heard anything of a white young lady with a child travelling with them. He was willing to do some inquiries for us as discreetly as possible. Should there be any news he would get word to us as quickly as he was able.

While everyone was outside, Imogene and I cleared the dishes. As we did so, I brought up the subject of my friend Mary. I tried to explain Mary's story asking that they be as discreet as possible as I asked for their help. We were still too new to the community to do this without the help of our friends. She understood. Imogene also reminded me that

Mary would now be wearing the Native clothing as well as having her hair in braids. By now I was sure she spoke Cree fluidly as would her daughter Ashenee. If I was to find my friend I was also going to need some help from God. I would need a lot of help. Imogene and I both knew we would pray for Mary daily.

Soon it was time for the late midday meal and what a feast it was. While the others stomped the snow off their boots, removed their hats and parkas I helped Imogene with the last minute preparations. Melvin quickly carved the chicken, which was the size of a small turkey, and smelled twice as good with its rich brown skin over the juicy meat. Boiled potatoes with cooked carrots and garden peas gave us much to give thanks for. Ginger nut cookies, hot coffee, and milk for the kinder rounded out our meal.

As we sat at the table together feeling so content, we each spoke of being so grateful to have found each other, now we both had a family nearby.

Before clearing the table Fritz and Katrin each received a surprise just for them. Melvin had made a wood spin top for each to play with. Imogene made them each a pair of winter socks, blue for Fritz and red for Katrin. How happy they were as they hugged them both with their thanks. Now it was time to put on parkas and hats, hitch up the team and head for home where chores were waiting. As we climbed into our sleigh we received one more gift for the trip home. Imogene had made fresh doughnuts that morning. How could we possibly get hungry again?

As Buck and Misty steadily pulled our rickety sleigh over the frozen snow we each sat quietly savouring our delicious memory of this special day. Fritz liked his top the best while Katrin thought her socks were the prettiest she had ever seen. They were both full of funny short stories of both Sandy and Pepper. I knew they were wishing they too had a pony but knew not to ask. For me it was my time spent with Imogene leaving me with memories I shall always treasure. After some careful thought, Floyd said his favourite was the ginger nut cookies. They tasted just like the ones my mother baked. Now it was time for a few happy tears as we settled in for the rest of the ride home.

As we rode along in silence we met a couple other sleighs travelling along this barren road. Just as I was thinking that I am glad there are no animals out today, our team each gave a couple snorts with ears straight up in alert. There at the edge of the bushes were two black bears watching the travellers going by. I was hoping they did not smell the food in our sleigh as I heard Fritz quietly saying, "Please do not come for my doughnut". We kept going at an even pace keeping my eye on them as we passed. They soon lost interest and went back into the forest.

Other than the magpies in the bushes calling to each other, a couple coyotes were the only other animals out in the cold brisk air. As Floyd drove the team to the front of our house we started to laugh. We had had company while we were out. An igloo of snow had been built at the door to greet us. Who could it have been? Floyd said since there was room to open the door, we should leave it for a couple days for the kinder to play in. Through squeals of joy I assured them it could stay for a couple days. Such fun they would have.

Chapter Twenty-One

That evening Floyd mentioned to me of another farmer Melvin had spoken of. They lived north west of town, which meant they would be closer to us. It seems most every time Melvin went to town during harvesting season, he would meet Marvin Faust there at the grain elevators, owned by the Saskatchewan Wheat Pool. He told of how he had a wife and two daughters. As the Faust family were Lutherans too, they would be able to tell us where the services were held. Melvin and his family attended the Catholic church in town. Melvin had suggested they visit us one day before most everyone became snowed in with the roads being impassable much of the time. Now we began to look forward to meeting another family.

For the next while the sun continued to shine brightly but the wind still blew making snow drifts everywhere freezing during the night. With the snow not piling as high on the west side of our log home due to the closeness of the willow trees, we piled snow against the wall for insulation. I would never have guessed I would help to make the snow deeper. It now was so deep it hid any sign of our rail fences surrounding our little farm. As we had no extra building for the harvesting machines they remained lined up outside along the edge of the row of spruce trees that protected our home from the wide-open fields where the wind loved to blow. The plod and the harrows were now covered in snow. Only the uneven pattern in the snow held the secret hiding place for our combine, binder as well as other small equipment waiting to be used again in the spring.

Chapter Twenty-Two

As winter came once more with its days of bright blue skies, and sparkling nighttime stars shinning as brightly as the moon, it gave me false hope that Nature's wrath would not return. They seemed to never touch God's earth. I so frequently found myself in great awe of this majestic beauty.

It was but a few nights later I woke in our pitch black home to the sound of the windows rattling. Without getting up from my warm bed I knew this meant another blizzard was upon us. The sky would now be dark with the wind blowing furiously. How much more snow could possibly be dropped on us? Which way was the wind going to blow today and how hard? Will this mean my kinder will not be able to attend school to get their education? I must remain firm and insist they be able to make a better life for themselves. They will need a life where they will have enough to eat, warm clothes to wear and a warm house to live in. I can hardly stand to see my family barely having enough food to eat. The kinder going to bed crying because they still want something more to eat. Here they will survive, but just so.

I easily filled the cold winter days baking bread, cooking meals and doing my outside chores. Floyd would help me with mine as I had the extra inside tasks. Any extra minutes I had I would spend mending socks, sewing underclothes for my growing kinder as I frequently looked outside the window in hopes of someone coming to pay us a visit.

Imogene gave me old sweaters to unravel and knit again for my children. Sitting on his bed, Fritz would not too happily wrap the yarn into a ball for me, winding it so tight it would bounce. I wondered if he really did not know what the word loose meant, or perhaps he was just too young. Maybe in his mind he though if he wrapped it too tight he wouldn't have to do it again. That wouldn't work. I did not have a pattern so I just added stitches and decreased stitches where I thought I needed to. It always worked as my homemade sweaters seemed to fit quite well bringing smiles to their faces eagerly waiting to wear them to school.

During the winter months Floyd was able to get a little extra rest in the stillness of the afternoons. I too would try to take a short rest a couple afternoons each week, but with my added winter chores it did not always happen. I had been trying to better my reading ability as well. With very little time when spring thaw came until the next winter season was upon us, I felt I just needed to make the time. The old newspapers Imogene had given me were just perfect. As I sat at the table in the evenings with the coal oil lamp burning barely giving me enough light to read, I felt it was slowly improving. I also needed to keep up with my arithmetic. I would need both for a better and easier life. Each time I thought of leaving the farm, it saddened me to know that the man I had married would give up so easily. Somehow I need to show him that we all deserve an easier and better life or we just will not survive, only exist.

One mild Sunday afternoon I heard the sound of a sleigh passing along the road. The sounds of strange horses came closer and closer. Soon it was close enough to see four people nearing our house with their red painted sleigh pulled by two large grey horses with their heads lowered as if to keep their eyes on the snowy path ahead.

Floyd put his boots and parka on, and then went outside to greet our visitors. Could it be the Faust family? We both hoped it was.

As I looked out the window I saw Floyd shaking hands with the gentleman driving the team. We did not know these people. Then he helped a smiling lady from the sleigh followed by two girls. As I opened the door to invite them into the warmth of our home, I felt the presence of a very warm and friendly lady with pretty freckles on her nose and cheeks. Once again I was overcome with joy. While Fritz and you Katrin, were shy so were their girls, Carmen and Grace.

When coats were removed, our guests seated, I put the coffee pot on. With only having four chairs, the four children sat on the beds until they became more comfortable on the floor to play snakes and ladders, our only board game. Bertha brought with them a loaf of fresh baked bread. I had just made butter the day before, for this I was grateful. As I excused myself to go outside the door to bring the butter in from the window box where it kept cold in a pail during the day, she said that was where they too kept a few items so they would not have to go to the well for it. It was easy to see that

Bertha and I would quickly become friends as we chatted as though we had known each other for many years. Feeling that they lived as we did soon gave me a more comfortable feeling.

Bertha wore a dark green dress over her short plump body that seemed to bounce with energy as she walked. She quickly expressed how her and Marvin were anxious to meet friends, as they too were fairly new to this northern community. Perhaps this would help us both to feel better with our families so far away. I secretly hoped that Marvin and Floyd would be compatible as well. Yes, they knew where the Lutheran Church was located as this is where they attended.

When the men came in, Floyd introduced me to Marvin with a big smile adding how he was going to like this man. Marvin was a slim built man with a sharp nose and a head of thick black curly hair that made his friendly dark eyes appear even darker. As Bertha and I looked at each other wondering what that was about, he stated that Marvin named his horses Buck and Missy. With that they both laughed as though it was the funniest thing there could be. It was easy to see that they not only thought the same but also had the same sense of humour. A look of understanding passed between Bertha and I just knowing what the other was thinking; an extended family in the making.

As we sat at the table enjoying our coffee with fresh baked bread, the children sat on the floor talking and laughing about school as they too enjoyed their bread with griebenschmalz. This was a treat for them. It was then that I felt I needed to call them children, not kinder. I must remember.

Much too soon it was time for them to leave for their farm where chores were waiting. Marvin said that Missy was not as happy walking with the wind and sleet blowing into her face as Buck is. With her even temper she will shake her head every once in a while to show her dislike as she tromped along pulling her share of the weight. Even the children were not ready to part just yet. With promises of us visiting them in a couple weeks, weather permitting, their whines turned to smiles. With you, Katrin being so shy, you had just started to enjoy yourself. For you we all felt bad the visit could not have been longer but there would be a next time as soon as possible.

That evening as we all did our chores the mild bright day began to fade. As a curtain of darkness began to cover the sky, it became darker with the air cooler soon turning into a cold wind blowing harder and harder until it was whipping the snow around us. I found myself praying that the Faust family would have made it home safely. When the wind blows so hard it is not a good time to be on the roads. Should the team stray to one side they could easily slip off the road into the snow filled ditch taking the sleigh and family with them. Too often this had happened. I knew Floyd too was worried. He displayed the sign of a man that was far away in thought unaware of the world around him.

That evening as we all warmed ourselves near the stove filled with crackling wood, we shared thoughts and feelings of our new friends. We were all excited at having new friends to share some time with, even though it will not be as often as we would like. Now it was time for bible stories for Fritz and Katrin, prayers and into bed for them. While they settled down under their grey wool army blankets I read to Floyd in our German bible. By now the wind was howling from the storm that was now upon us. The sky was black as far as the eye could see. Jack Frost will once again visit our home as we sleep the night away. As I closed my eyes I hoped that Big Red would sleep just a little longer in the morning.

As I sat near the stove to keep warm while I did some mending, with the wood snapping, I was once again thinking of our life in the north. As we were only able to listen to our battery-operated radio for a half hour each week, there was little to distract my mind from my many concerns. I had tried so hard to be content with the quiet evenings, but many times it reminded me of how much I missed my siblings. During the winter months we were snowed into our small farm most of the time. It was both scary and difficult for the children to walk to school for the education they needed.

Making the trip to town occasionally for the supplies we were not able to grow, became extremely difficult. The winter months were growing longer and longer. Each day when I looked out the window, it seemed the snow banks were deeper than the day before. We were both accustomed to long hard days of work but nothing like this. There were still wild animals roaming our land that was of much concern.

As I sat deep in my own thoughts, I wondered how much more we could endure. I knew in my heart of hearts that I could not bear to make this my forever home. I would work hard to find a means of moving away where life could be a little better. My determination to save extra pennies and nickels was even stronger now. I just needed to find that way. Having to go out into the bitter cold today to hang laundry on the line filled me with even more desire to leave for an easier life. Having to wash and scrub the clothes and bedding on a scrub board with the wash tub sitting on the back of the stove to stay hot, would sometimes bring tears to my eyes. I had long since learned that I needed to work like a man, which I knew I did, but sometimes it just seemed too much. Each time I mentioned this to Floyd he put his head down becoming sullen as he stared at the floor beneath his feet. Regardless of the bitter outdoor weather, he would dress in his only pair of boots and winter parka stomping outside to be alone in the barn area talking to Buck. He would not even discuss any possibility of needing more or an education for the children. He had not learned to read or write and was doing just fine, they will too he would say.

"What is wrong with this life? Why can we not all just stay here?"

Time and again he would angrily say these same words over and over to me. I tried to assure him that while farming was a good life, this was just too far north and desolated. We worked so hard and long for the little we reaped. The days were just too long and hard. Some days I felt I just could not take another. I knew he thought when we became too old our children would be there to help out. I knew this farm could not support two families. Dear Lord, what will I do?

Chapter Twenty-Three

It was weeks before there was any sign of this harsh weather calming itself. By now the horses could barely stomp through the deep snow. I was beginning to lose my battle with the children going to school for fear they would get lost along the way. As we had no schoolbooks at home, I tried to help them read the newspaper, but even many words were too big and strange for me. We had no paper or pencils at home for them to write. When I took them outside to do chores I would stop by a snow bank for a short while so we could all practice our printing. A piece of kindling made a good pencil. The next time we would practice our arithmetic. Together we sang the few children's songs I knew over and over again. It was so still during the day in the winter months that we could hear the bush rabbits running about between the trees.

Just when the loneliness of being trapped on the farm for days on end was becoming too much, there was a break in the weather. I could once again see signs of things being a little brighter. It was now time to see the spring thaw just around the corner. The icicles on the roof's edge began to thaw in the afternoon sunshine dripping their cold water on the snow below. As the snow began to gradually melt, it left a reminder of the water that would soon be covering the fields and garden area. The ditches will be overflowing. What a beautiful sight it is, but first there is still much snow to leave.

When Saturday came Floyd suggested that if

the next day was promising to be a pleasant day for driving the snow covered roads, we should take a trip to visit the Faust family. We all needed a little time away from the farm. I could not have agreed more. My heart lifted.

When morning came with the darkness slowly making way for the sun's early light, my heart rose with high anticipation of the day ahead. Jack Frost had not visited our home last night, but it would still be cold and crisp outside. The sky showed all the signs of sunshine to help keep us warm as we travelled.

By mid morning we were climbing into our sleigh packed with an extra blanket to huddle under for the children when they became cold as well as a loaf of bread I had baked the day before. Whenever they would start to feel cold I would have them run behind for a while to warm their feet, then they would stand on the runners for a few minutes of fun with the breeze blowing in their faces leaving them with rosy cheeks.

After we travelled a couple miles we turned east, another half mile further we saw what we had feared. It was clear that by the churned up snow leaving the icy road, a sleigh had slid off into the deep ditch. The tracks appeared to be those of a sleigh, not horses. That was a good sign. For this we were thankful.

As we traveled further we came upon a young man walking along the hard packed frozen road. As he limped along we wondered why he was out in this cold so far from his home, at least there was no sight of one. Upon offering him a ride he climbed into our sleigh expressing his gratefulness for the help. He readily explained that he had been going to visit a friend when his horse was spooked by a coyote throwing him onto the side of the road landing with a hard thud on his backside. He was sure that by now Horse would be standing at the corral waiting for him to return.

He spoke of his family. His pa was not too well due to trouble breathing especially during the cold winter months. His ma would become so tired from doing so many chores that she crawled into bed as soon as possible staying there until Charlie crowed in the morning. Both his older sisters had married at age fourteen and moved away. This farm had the sign of a very meagre existence. It was so small that it nestled into a clump of trees as though it was hiding from the outside world. It appeared to be held together by the branches of the leafless trees surrounding it.

From the cautious way his parents spoke it was clear they were neither accustomed to company or comfortable with someone seeing their little shack they called home. It was nothing more than a tiny small mud hut with slabs that appeared to have been there without repair for many years. Sometime later we were to learn that this young lad slept in the barn with the animals. Their one cow appeared to be so undernourished Floyd felt she would hardly be able to provide enough milk for their needs. I knew I must convince Floyd that we visit these people as soon as the weather would allow. Perhaps the only help we might give would be a loaf of bread and some companionship, should it be accepted. We must try. I wondered if anyone even knew they lived there.

Eventually we reached the farm of our new friends that we were seeking. What a beautiful farm it was. It was much larger than ours. The buildings were all painted a fresh red with white trim. Now I knew why the sleigh was red. They even had a small miniature house for Johnny, their farm hand. Later we were to learn that Johnny had hopped a ride on the train a few years earlier to head north in hopes of finding work. When he found this was the end of the railway line he took his bag and began walking west until he came to a farm. Here he would ask for room and board in exchange for work. While he thought of himself as a man, Bertha told me he was just an older school boy willing to do a man's work. On the condition that he would study his reading and arithmetic in the evenings, he could stay. He happily did as he remembered his father telling him it was time for him to find his own way in the world. Johnny knew they just could not afford to feed their ten kids. The three eldest just had to leave home, and he was the oldest. His two sisters would find work doing housework or perhaps as a chambermaid at the local hotel.

Four years have now passed with Johnny being almost one of the family. He worked hard each and every day. Once in a while he would agree to join the Faust family for dinner. It seemed he preferred to be alone. They still did not know if he had a family or what his last name was, or where he came from. For that matter they questioned whether his name was really Johnny. With the fear of him striking out alone again, they decided not to question him too much giving him reason to leave. At least here he would be warm and sheltered. With Johnny there, Bertha did not have to do many outside chores.

As we sat in their kitchen enjoying our visit we explained of our encounter with a polite reserved young man. Marvin was sure he knew of the family. If this was the family he was thinking of, his pa had some other illness leaving his Mrs. to do most of the chores. Bertha said they were poorer than dirt. She also said she would take an extra large loaf of bread rather than two. She had heard that they were proud people not wanting a hand out from anyone. They would stop in soon to just say hello making no sign of wishing to enter their home making them feel more uncomfortable.

As the children ran around the farm with Carmen and Grace meeting all their animals, we enjoyed a delightful visit indoors near the warmth of the cook stove. It seemed we had just arrived when it was time to bring the children inside for Fritz and you, Katrin to warm up for the trip home. With a delicious meal of home-made sausage, pickles and bread served on their large wood table with a blue flowered oil cloth, it was time to offer our thanks and appreciation as we prepared to leave for home where chores were waiting for us.

As we travelled towards our log home we felt the temperature begin to drop as the breeze picked up. The faces of Buck and Misty began to have a white tinge as though they had aged during the afternoon. Floyd pulled the hood of his parka a little tighter as he guided our faithful team along the frozen snow covered road. The children sat on the floor of the sleigh with the blanket pulled tight around them and over their heads. I stood near the front keeping a watchful eye for any signs of anything moving ahead that might frighten the horses.

As I watched the darkness slowly descend upon us, I began to sing the songs I knew my family enjoyed. Floyd would join in every once in a while. It was as though we were sleighing in a winter wonderland, but this one held many dangers to be aware of.

As we became closer to our next neighbours farm, we could hear the howl of the grey wolves. There must be mule deer lingering nearby in the bushes. Wolves do not eat humans or rarely attack us, that is just a legend or preconception. Still, it is an eerie sound on a cold night on the open land. While I did not like the idea of them killing the deer, I knew it was nature's way of maintaining a balance in the animal population, as well as to feed themselves.

As we drove past our barn Floyd said he felt something was not right, just what he did not know. I scanned the bushes but could see no sign of anything amiss. The horses were relaxed as they meandered to the front of the house as though they could do this in their sleep.

After Floyd and I took a careful look around, we checked the inside of the house. All was as we had left it earlier. There were no new tracks to be seen around the yard. Where had his uneasiness come from? This was not like him.

Leaving the children in the house we drove to the barn to check on our cattle. As we walked past the chicken house carrying our kerosene lantern, I took special note if each pen was filled as usual. No problem there. Daisy was standing in the middle of the pen with her head down, not moving. Had one of her young ones become ill? When we took a closer look we found that she had a bush rabbit in front of her. It is not usual for them to enter into the farm area; perhaps this young one was just too inquisitive or extra hungry. Had Daisy killed it or had it died of fright? Either way she had no idea what to do with it now that it was hers and hers alone.

Daisy was known to be a gentle sow but when Floyd attempted to remove her catch she became irritated, clearly showing her aggression. After spending a couple minutes gently talking to her he felt he could now move closer. He took two steps closer when she angrily moved to attack him. We decided it best that I draw her away with the enticement of some food. Soon the temptation was too much for her. She gingerly moved toward my bucket of food as I slowly led her further away. While Daisy was eating her full, Floyd removed her catch. She looked at us as if to say 'what is your problem, I have no problem'.

As the snow began to melt a little more each day, we all felt that we were not so trapped away from the rest of the world. A couple weeks later Mother Nature had another surprise in store. We woke to freezing sleet and snow coming down so hard we could hardly brave the harsh beating on our faces as we headed to the barn for morning chores. The water filled snow banks were now becoming sheets of shiny ice. The animals would need to be kept in the barn until it began to melt again. No one in the community would be going outside unless it was to do their chores.

It was a few days before this nasty weather began to change once more. First we woke to a feeling of stillness outside. The wind had finally subsided. The morning sky was slowly rising up in a brighter blue with patches of soft yellow and oranges giving a new light to the day ahead. Once again the snow began to thaw, the icicles began to drip its cold water on the snow below, and the community once more came alive with feelings of hope in their hearts and minds.

Chapter Twenty-Four

With school classes in session once again a regular schedule resumed. It was time for the community to gather for a social evening at the Little School House. I was so excited to see our neighbours just to be sure everyone was well. Both Floyd and I feared that some had not survived as well as we had.

Finally the big Saturday evening came. Buck and Misty were left to wait near the barn for us with other teams. As usual, the men gathered on one side eager to talk of their farms, the children played on another side with the women gathering together for feminine chatter.

We spoke of winter sewing and mending, baking and caring for our children during this harsh winter. We shared any news we had of others having difficulty that may need a helping hand, perhaps some food. We also spoke of Miss Beulah praising her for her strength as she cared for herself during this difficult time with little help from others.

Chopping her wood was a task that was shared by the older boys in the school, but with the oldest being twelve the adults checked on it too whenever they were nearby. All the students helped to pile the wood close to her small home that sat nearby the Little School House. This brave young lady was showing remarkable courage and maturity for one so young living alone with no one to protect her. With no one for company, it was a good thing teachers like to read.

As the men shared what they each knew of others, plans were made to help those in need. One farm north of the school had been hit even harder by this fierce winter than the remainder of the community.

Due to their barn already having been in desperate need of repairs, a section of the roof had collapsed leaving room for the snow to fall next to the cow stalls, some overflowing into the horse area. Their mule was limping as he was led out for water. Perhaps he slipped on the frozen flooring. Their two milk cows appeared to be cold but otherwise not injured. Their only horse was not eating well but showed no sign of being physically injured. It was agreed that on Monday, if weather permitted travelling, they would have a work bee to help these quiet people pull through this extra load the winter had left with them. Someone mentioned having noticed the barn door barely closing the last time he stopped by. No sense leaving an easy invitation for a wild animal in search of food. The men would discreetly check on the house while they were there.

Miss Beulah reported that one family had not sent their children to school for three weeks. Could someone find a way to check on them too? As they had seven children, a couple ladies offered to each send a loaf of bread along.

The evening was spent with talk of how we could help each other. No one had it in their heart to dance or sing. There was too much difficulty in our community needing our help. A plan needed to be made.

As the evening grew on with darkness having set long ago, the children sound asleep on the desks they studied from; someone mentioned that another family with fourteen children were also struggling. Talk was that their eldest son had not returned home one day. His parents thought he had gone to school. Upon checking the register, Miss Beulah confirmed that he had not arrived nor had he since then.

As we lived closest, Floyd went to check with the family to find that no one had gone out searching for him on that cold day. His father was not aware that he was gone, nor did he seem to be worried with the news, he already had too much to do. His mother said she thought if he did not go to school, he had probably gone to find work and would one day come home but was not concerned. As at age thirteen he was too old to attend country school and having not completed his studies, it was not likely he had made his way to town nine miles away. His mother assured Floyd her family was fine and did not require any assistance.

Floyd returned that day with a heavy heart. He was a compassionate and caring man in his quiet and reserved way. He never did wish to meddle in other people's business, but when it came to children I could see the added weight on his worried shoulders.

The next day I went to visit Miss Beulah with what little information we had. As he was now over the age of twelve, the School Board would have no interest in his whereabouts.

Floyd said he had a feeling that he was taking up with a family needing a little help or else a large family that was not aware he was staying with them. Or perhaps like many young men, actually boys, he had hopped the train in search of food and shelter elsewhere.

This was a common practice that was illegally done by hundreds of men and some women, mostly men that came to be known as hoboes. Hoboes would beg for food at farmhouses, sometimes being turned away. Many were killed by accidents or by the brutal railroad "bulls" hired by the railroad to ensure that only paying customers were aboard. Because of the bulls they knew they needed to board outside of the railroad yard, running along side as the train gained speed grabbing a hold and jumping into open boxcars. The young boys were not fully aware of the dangers and so many fell or were pushed to their death. It was both an excitement and desperation they did not fully understand.

Sometime later Miss Beulah had taken our offer of a ride to town with us. She would need a few things from the General Store. The General Store was located in the heart of town on Main Street. Each morning Mr. Bosh would sweep the uneven slab sidewalk in front with a corn broom. During the winter a shovel was used to clear most of the snow away to make walking safe for his customers.

It seemed every inch of his store was stocked with all things needed by a family. Just inside the door on the left, was the area for fruit, vegetables and candy just at the right height to tempt the children. My children's favourite was the stand with many coloured lollipops beside the glass jar filled with bubble gum. I feel so bad they were not able to have money to spend.

The right hand side of the store was stocked with clothing for all members of a family. Hats, suspenders and ties for men and boys were hung on the wall. Ladies' hats, aprons and towels looked pretty on a shelf. Along the back wall on the left hand side, was a small area stacked to the ceiling with pails, shovels, hammers, nails and some white wash paint, lanterns and lamps.

The right hand side was for the ladies. A cabinet against the wall was filled with all colours of threads, thimbles, and needles. There was also yarn, crochet hooks and knitting needles. There were bolts of pretty coloured cotton fabrics for dresses, shirts and curtains. There was also an area large enough for three or four ladies to stand to chat with one another where they were able to be out of the cold. I so enjoyed my time on each trip to town in this friendly store.

As we travelled along she shared what little she knew of this family of nine that chose to keep to themselves. Their oldest child was a frail outspoken girl eleven years of age but had the responsibility of an adult since she was eight years old. It seems she was the one to bake the bread and care for her younger siblings along with other chores. Her ten-year-old brother was wild and difficult to handle. He chose not to listen to anyone especially his older sister and mother. At school, when he did go, his language was so bad she constantly had to reprimand him. Miss Beulah had sent several notes home but had the feeling they were not read by either parent. Perhaps they were not able to read. When the children did come to school they often had no lunch so she fed them a slice of bread and butter or lard, which ever she had.

During the social evening she requested a member of the School Board to visit with her regarding this family. She was at her wits end with these unruly dirty children that seemed to only create trouble with her other students. To what extent was her responsibility, she did not know. It would be another week before someone from the City of Cold Cut would arrive.

Chapter Twenty-Five

It was just over a month later when the Faust family visited us one mild Sunday afternoon. The roads were still not at their best but not nearly so dangerous. It was a time to catch up on each other's life from the harsh winter.

We were so relieved to hear that they had very little problems due to the storms. However, we were saddened to hear that a family near them was not so lucky. The strong winds had blown through their farm taking with it the roof off their house as well as ripping away a part of a wall on their barn leaving the animals exposed and vulnerable. Their buildings were older and not so sturdy, leaving them to be an easy target for the harsh storms.

Marvin asked Johnny if he would ride over to a few of the neighbours asking for help for this kind family. In minutes Johnny had mounted their dapple-grey horse, Star, and was off. Soon there was a work bee in progress. Split logs and spare slabs were brought as well as nails and hammers. The men worked quickly taking no time for idle chatter. There was too much at stake.

Having repaired many a building before it seemed it was no time until the men had once again secured the barn. The animals would be safe once more from the hungry wild life lurking around waiting for something to eat.

Just as quickly they began to repair the roof on the small house sitting beside a grove of birch trees. As he thanked the men, Mr. Schubert assured them they could now manage. The family would sleep in the barn until he had the roof repaired. Marvin assured him that was not what neighbours did. By now the work crew were well on their way to securing their home as well. A look of relief swept over Mr. Schubert's face that had shown many signs of a life of hard work in the outdoors. He clearly was not one to ask for help.

As the men happily worked together it did not take long until they were gathering their hammers to head home with many grateful thanks from Mr. Schubert on behalf of himself and his family.

Before leaving Marvin thought he would say hello to Mrs. Schubert who was waiting in a nearby shed with the rest of the family. As he neared the door he heard some crying as though someone was wincing with pain. Marvin quickly knocked on the door and walked in. There he found her lying on the floor with three pairs of frightened eyes watching him. He quickly learned from the oldest child that she had been hit on the head from some debris as it came flying down landing on her. He asked that one of the children find their father to come to the shed so they could talk. Perhaps Mr. Schubert was not aware that his wife was bleeding from the top of her head.

As Mr. Schubert came in, it was obvious to Marvin that he had not known of the situation. His Mrs. had done a good job of concealing her injuries. After being assured that none of his children were hurt, he insisted he check her injuries as they quietly spoke to each other.

As she was awake and coherent, like many people they did not wish to see the doctor. This cost money, which they just, did not have. After sending his eight-year-old daughter to the house to prepare the bed, he waited a couple minutes before picking his wife up and carrying her into the house to rest in their own straw bed.

Marvin assured him that he would bring Bertha around in the morning to see if they could be of help. He knew she would bake some fresh bread. Mr. Schubert said he was sure they would manage just fine while Marvin felt he really wanted to say how much he would like that, he was just too proud.

Soon Marvin and Johnny were on their way home. Johnny explained that while he was waiting he checked their fencing. A section of it near the barn had also been ripped apart leaving it totally unsafe for the animals. It was a split log fence that had been there for many years. Some of the barbed wire gate would also need replacing. They agreed to hold another farmer's work bee. Like many others they would just show up with hammer and nails.

It seemed the storms blew through their area much more severely than our area a little further north. It reminded me of how fortunate we ourselves were. Now it was time for my next question, had they heard anything more of an Indian tribe returning. Both Marvin and Bertha thought there was going to be one returning to the empty Native land closer to our place in the early spring. I immediately felt my excitement rising. We were not sure that we would be welcome uninvited on their land. Perhaps on a trip to town I would see my friend Mary.

Then we spoke of the young lad from our community that had left home. They did not know of a farmer in their community having suddenly taken on a young hand. Marvin would ask Johnny. While he seldom went to town, he was also very closed lipped. Somehow we felt little assurance of any information. He could be miles away with the sound of the train chugging along just a memory as he listened to the forlorn call of the whistle as they entered a lonely town. The brakes would hiss and screech as the train slowly came to a stop, his time to wake up to survey the new area. If he was somewhere within a day's drive, he would likely return home by fall. If not he was not apt to return for many years, if ever, as he makes his life elsewhere and a family of his own like many other young men have done.

As we bid our friends farewell the sky was beginning to turn darker over us leaving the trees to send a cooler breeze in its path. As I did my chores after returning home, my mind went over and over the conversation Bertha and I had of our lives as homesteaders. It did nothing to change my mind that I should continue to find a way to move on.

Several days later as I began to bake bread I thought of our trip to visit the Faust family. How fortunate we were to have travelled there and back with no mishaps over the poor roads that were never maintained. They were as nature gave them to us either covered in snow and ice or mud and deep dirty ruts. I know that I must try hard to see the beauty in this northern land that barely keeps my family alive for as long as I continue to live here.

Right about then I found myself desperately desiring one of Bertha's delicious cookies. Ever since we headed north I have been yearning for the day when I would have the ingredients to bake a batch of cookies. Just one batch for Christmas is all I ask. As my tears began to flow I reprimanded myself for wishing for something that was not about to happen. There is so much comfort in eating just one tasty cookie.

"Katrin, did you know that the first record of cookies was that of test cakes to test the oven temperature?" This was a few hundred years ago when they were baked in wood stoves and almost always called teacakes. Today there are hundreds of cookie recipes having their own cookbooks instead of just a page in the back of a cookbook. This is just a snippet of useless information I thought you might be interested in. I know you Katrin, love both eating and baking them as much as I do.

Joe tells me friends have been baking for them. Bruce and Dawn always say thank you and do enjoy them but not near as much as the ones you bake. I know they like Grandma's cookies too, but moms are always better. It is time that you woke up and started enjoying cookies with your young ones.

Chapter Twenty-Six

The remainder of my day was just like the others. When I set the dough to rise, I would go outside and do chores until it was time to make lunch for Floyd and I. You and your brother had taken your lard sandwiches to school again. At least now the weather was mild enough for your lunch to not freeze before you arrived. After lunch I would do indoor chores until it was time to bake the bread. Just because I was feeling so sad, I saved some of the dough to fry in lots of lard as a treat for you and Fritz having them hot and fresh. Because it was a day that I knew we all needed something extra to boost our spirits, I made two for each including your dad and I.

Before I began to make dinner I went to the barn to do the milking. With my forehead leaning against Bossy, sitting on my old three-legged milk stool that was once my mothers, I found tears began to flow once again. This time I just could not stop them.

It was weeks later before my spirits began to lift, but just a little. It seemed as though Mother Nature did not have any kindness in her heart for us. One day we would enjoy a bright blue sky with barely any wisps of clouds to be seen when the next would descend upon us with dark skies filled with icy water just waiting to pour down on us. She would let out a couple of loud claps to be followed by the giant roar of thunder. Minutes later we would receive a torrential downpour of heavy cold rain mixed with wet snow. This only lasted for a short while, but was enough to overload the already saturated ground.

By morning the ditches, now filled to overflowing, were forcing their way through the wet dirt road leaving behind its path of swift flowing dirty water. Now the school children would need to jump over this newly made ditch until the water lowered itself for the farmers to fill it in. In the meantime, it was a great place for them to float sticks seeing which one would travel the fastest and go the longest distance without getting caught on some debris.

A few weeks later I found I still needed some female company to help me to lift my spirits, if not for me for my family. It was time to invite Miss Beulah to our house for a visit. She must be feeling shut in too. Everyone agreed this would be nice for us all.

Fritz and Katrin were always happy to walk the mile to the school to extend our invitation returning with their teacher in tow. While during school hours they had to pretend they hardly knew her, they now felt this was a special guest they were just too happy to chatter away with.

When they tired of the excitement of 'teacher' they went off to play in the bushes. Floyd returned to the barn leaving us time to chat together. Much to my surprise she was quick to tell me that she had been seeing a fine young gentleman from the next community. He had been coming to visit her one day each weekend all winter long. And we thought the weather had kept everyone home. He must be real sweet on her to travel this distance on horseback under such challenging conditions. No one knew, she laughed.

A couple weeks later Fritz came home from school proudly carrying a note in his lunch pail from Miss Beulah. I could not read fast enough with two pairs of eyes beside me trying to peek. With one look at me, they knew it was good news. I could not keep the smile from my face.

What does it say, please tell us? First one then the other begging now, now. First I need to read it to your dad and then I will share it with you, I reminded them. One look at the long faces I quickly said "lets go find your dad in the barn." By the time I was out the door they were at the corral calling Floyd.

After sharing her note with the others, and giving a reminder that this was just for our family, not the other students, we went back to our routine of filling the evenings with chores.

A few weeks later my spirits were beginning to wane once more when Fritz came home from school with another note in his lunch pail. To my great joy there was to be a Ladies Aid meeting the coming Saturday. We, Katrin and I, were invited. Of course we will attend.

Finally Saturday came with the family bathing in the morning instead of the afternoon. I prepared lunch a little earlier so as to have time to clean up dishes before changing into my blue dress.

As we entered the Little School House I could

hear the wonderful chatter of the ladies greeting each other. In a short while the meeting was called to order with eleven ladies and one Katrin, present. After a briefing on the community Miss Beulah asked for a minute to speak. I am sure most thought she was going to leave her teaching position with us. Quietness fell over the room with all eyes to the front.

Taking a deep breath, and then a soft laugh she quickly assured everyone that she had no plans to move on just now. She loved this community and her students but she now had another love in her life. When the clapping subsided she told of how a young gentleman had been visiting her since early last fall. Now the chatter began, did you know? How come I did not know? And so on. After a few minutes everyone was asked to listen to what Beulah had to say.

She went on to say that she would only be staying until school closed for the summer. Then there would be a wedding at which time she would need to move to another community where she would be a working farmer's wife. That was something that was new to all. What kind of a man was she to marry? Who was he and which community? No one knew a farmer's wife that worked out of the farm.

Beulah then changed the conversation to her students and their progress, staying safely away from her personal life. As always there were some that just would not pass if they did not pull up their marks. They must be able to read at their level, write and do arithmetic for their level or they must be held back.

She asked for some extra help cleaning the schoolroom once a month, at least until the weather dried up. Each day she would ask students to clean the blackboard and brushes before leaving for home. Sometimes an unruly student was asked to remain indoors during afternoon recess for this chore. Then she explained her reluctance to do this as they then were that much more rambunctious for the remainder of the afternoon. She was aware that they all had chores to get home for. A few mothers said their children could take their turn helping out. Another mother and myself offered to help with the extra cleaning. We would bring our children to help us.

As soon as Beulah sat back down we were told there was some very sad news from the next community. On Tuesday after school a eight year old girl was outside playing with her siblings. Suddenly Anna started to scream holding her head as she fell down on the ground. Her younger brother ran to the house calling for their mother to come quick. Like only a mother can do, she was there in an instant. One look at her tiny daughter laying face down barely breathing, she sent this little boy to run as fast as he could to the field to fetch his father.

Not being able to understand what his frightened son was saying through his tears, he unhitched his horse from the stone boat, mounted and headed for the house. Not until he was nearly there did he remember himself that he had left his little son standing in the wide-open field by himself.

As he knelt beside Anna he could see a slight movement in her tiny chest. She was still alive. He would need to take her to the town hospital eight and a half miles away as quickly as possible.

He quickly mounted his already weary horse to make the urgent trip to town. As soon as his wife lifted Anna into his arms and covered her with a jacket, he turned Whiskey around and headed for the road.

Holding Anna ever so tightly against his body so as to not drop her or have there be too much movement for her to bear, he knew he needed to ride in one with Whiskey. With only his legs to hold his balance on Whiskey's wide back, he nudged him into a steady rhythm. In order to not waste time but also have a smoother ride for Anna, he chose a steady easy gallop.

In what seemed like hours, they came to the area known as the Muskeg, a wet grassy bog. To take this short cut he would need to have one of the children from their farm open and close the gate, usually wanting a penny for a lollipop on their next trip to town. What if there was no one near the edge of their field to see him? No, he could not take the chance; he would need to take the long way around.

Another two miles and he would be on the main road. He would then have to slow down to give Whiskey some time to regain his strength. There is a spot just before the turn that he would let him take a drink from the ditch if the footing was safe. He knew he just could not chance Whiskey slipping on the wet edge of the ditch.

As they hurried along with no sight of anyone else on the roads, his mind was heavy with worry for their dear little Anna. For the first time he was not aware of the steady chirping of the Magpies that usually became too noisy for him when he wanted solitude to collect his thoughts. He did not notice the mule deer watching them as they flew by.

As he slowed for the place he felt Whiskey could have a quick drink, a family returning from town pulled over to offer assistance. The gentleman quickly jumped down to give Whiskey a little urging, and to hurry him up. Not only did they not have the time to spare, he knew it would not be good for Whiskey to drink too much water. With a short thank you for their help, they turned onto the main road for the last leg of the trip. There would not be as many ruts so perhaps they could make even better time.

He was sure that he could still see little Anna breathing when they were stopped. On this road he would be able to leave it up to Whiskey to get them there while he talked to his little girl. The kind family that he did not know had said they would be praying for them. He too knew she was in God's hands. Surely He would not want such a sweet little one to go to Heaven so early.

As they raced through town along Main Street to the hospital he saw merchants and shoppers standing on the edge of the road to see who was coming in such a hurry. He knew they would be thinking there was going to be a robbery at the only bank in town.

With dust flying he pulled hard on the reins to bring Whiskey to an abrupt halt in front of the door to the hospital. A nurse in her white dress and cap came running out to help. Taking little Anna from his arms, she ran into the hospital calling for Doc. Brown to come quick.

As exhausted as he was, Mr. Stewart ran into the hospital trying desperately to catch up to nurse Minnie. She was just too fast for him. They were now in the operating room with Doc. Brown, and the door was closed.

Standing outside the door for what seemed like an hour, he decided to knock on the door. "Sit on a chair!" came the doctor's stern reply.

With no other choice he reluctantly sat on the old wood chair that had one arm missing from too much use.

It was some time before Doc. Brown came out only to go directly to his office, with not so much as a nod in his direction. What seemed like a long time later, Mr. Stewart was invited into the doctor's office. When the good doctor started with I am sorry to tell you this, Mr. Stewart said his heart fell as he began to shake. He heard bits and pieces only.

Is this my Anna he is speaking of? But I could not do anything to save her. Anna? She did not suffer. Who, Anna?

He heard Doc. Brown say I will be back shortly with some black coffee. Then we will talk again. Before the coffee came, Officer Judd arrived. He would need to ask some questions but first he extended his deepest sympathies to the family he had come to know so well.

Once again, Doc. Brown assured him there was nothing he could have done. Just one of those strange things that happens to some people just not usually a young child. Officer Judd would need to visit Mrs. Stewart in order to file a report with the Vital Statistics Registry in Cross Cut. Already they wanted to know which minister should they notify, which cemetery did he want his little girl to be buried in and even which day. This is all happening too fast.

A week later there was to be a funeral service for Anna in the Lutheran Church some ten miles west but we must go. Katrin needs to say goodbye to her friend.

After the long trip to the church, we gathered inside to hear the words of our Lord given by Reverend Klein. Following the singing of Jesus Loves Me the congregation was invited to go forward for their final farewell. Anna lay peacefully in a white dress looking like a sleeping angel on earth. For our family, this was a difficult moment but nothing compared to her parents. I felt my heart break as I watched my friend Anna being assisted to give her final farewell to her little Anna and namesake. I knew their lives would never be the same again. How could they?

The ride home was a sombre one. No one had anything to say. Not even the sight of the deer grazing beside the road or the chirp of the Magpies could steel our thoughts away from sweet little Anna.

Chapter Twenty-Seven

Seeding time was upon us once again. First the land had to be prepared. The endless amount of stones that seemed to surface each year needed to be picked and hauled away. Some days we felt that we were growing stones and roots for which there was no need. Manure needed to be spread and then plowed under making the soil dark and rich to grow the best possible crops. This our horses produced free of charge.

I had carefully saved the seeds from last year for our garden. The flower seeds would be planted around the outside edge of the large garden again. I was anxious to plant each year, then watch the little plants break through the soil in their straight rows. I did know that as I was excited to watch our garden grow, there would be much more work to come. The weeds needed to be pulled so as to not choke the plants, nor rob them of the soil's nutrients. Then it would be time to pick and can. This would soon be back breaking work that some days I would feel it too much to do along with the rest of my chores. This was life on the farm.

As soon as we felt we could spare a day away, we took a trip to town taking Miss Beulah with us. As we neared town she asked if Floyd and I would go to the feed store with her. There was someone there she wanted us to meet. Of course, four little ears were already wise. With a pleading look to Miss Beulah she invited them along as she hugged them both. They promised to not tell as they jumped up and down with excitement.

After Floyd tended to the horses, he met us by the Red and White Store at the edge of town. As we walked together he soon just had to ask, "Is there any chance that beautiful black stallion would be the one to bring your someone special to town? What do you think Fritz, have you seen a black horse at the Little School House? "

"Yes, one time we did, did we not Katrin?"

"The man just smiled at us," said Katrin followed by some giggles with Fritz joining in.

The look on Miss Beulah's face clearly said she had not known about this. Her secret had been out. It seems it is safe with Fritz and Katrin.

As we entered the feed store, a nice looking young man in his late twenties came towards us. Before greeting Miss Beulah he gave Fritz and Katrin a big smile.

"Well, young ones, we meet again," he said.

With that, Beulah quickly introduced us to her friend George West from Prairie Range Community. George was a husky dark haired young man of medium height with sparkling brown eyes and a friendly smile for all. Like many young farm men he wore overalls over a red plaid shirt with a straw hat. How handsome he looked. Just as the rosy look on Beulah's cheeks had begun to fade, George leaned over and kissed her on the cheek. This brought out the giggles. Even my stern look did nothing to end their fun.

Leaving us standing with Beulah, George took their hands and started to walk in the direction of the Red and White Store. Floyd and I both knew he had just impressed Beulah beyond measure. Us too.

In a couple minutes all three were back each enjoying the sweet taste of a red lollipop.

"Did anyone else want one?" George innocently asked looking from one to the other as though this was something he did all the time.

After a short visit we left them to chat while we went about our business in town. The next time George came to visit they would walk down to our farm for a cup of coffee. I just hope it will be when I have fresh bread baked, if not it will be biscuits with butter. I must remember to always keep a little flour on hand.

I went to the General Store to visit with any ladies that may be there from the nearby farms. Floyd went to the elevators to visit with the men. My children used their time to run around the town checking out the schoolyard as well as the ball diamond and every other place I did not know about. They just loved to be in town. They called it the best place on earth.

As I was visiting with Bertha and Ellie, Fritz and Katrin came running in to tell me there was a parcel at the small post office. There you could send and receive telegrams as well.

I was so excited that I nearly ran as fast as my children. We have not as yet, had any word from our families.

Much to my surprise there was a large cardboard box tied with a light rope to prevent any damage causing it's contents to fall out. It was from my sister Ursula. However did she find me? As it was too big and heavy for them to carry, I sent them to find their dad to pick it up before we leave for home. Now for the first time they wanted to go home right then. They knew I would not allow it to be opened in town, even though I was very tempted. Perhaps there is a letter from my dear sister. For now I will go back to the General Store to make the most of my time with my lady friends, it never is long enough. For me this too was a special time we ladies enjoyed.

Much too soon we were headed home with Buck and Misty leading the way. In a couple minutes the conversation turned to George. Fritz and Katrin were quiet now so as to not miss a word spoken. Perhaps it was more to hide the gum in their mouths that was forbidden off the farm. A treat from George, I was sure. As long as they were polite chewing with their mouths closed I pretended I had not seen a thing. I knew by the smell this was real gum, not the sap they had picked off the spruce trees that they usually chewed.

"So," asked Floyd in his usual direct but soft way, "any chance this George is the son of Stanley West from the West side of Prairie Range?"

"Yes, he is the one. His mother is Helen. He has four older brothers that no longer live at home. His younger sister Jeannie is still at home. She will be leaving in two years to study nursing."

"That is quite the spread they have. Bigger than the rest of the community together I hear. Hope he treats you well and not just with his means. You are a right nice lady."

After assuring us both that George is a real gentleman just like his father, she told of them having spoken of their plans for the future. A change was to be in store for the next fall. I knew what that meant. I could tell that Fritz understood and knew that he would tell Katrin as soon as they were alone. They were no secrets between them.

With talk of George, all thoughts had been lost of the parcel that my mind kept straying to. By the looks of the sun leaving us, and the air becoming cooler I knew it would be time to milk cows and make supper before I could even think of my precious parcel.

Chapter Twenty-Eight

It was time for Fritz and Katrin to get ready for bed and still I had not had time to open my parcel. They begged me to stop what I was doing so they could see too.

Carefully untying the string so as to be able to use it again, I carefully removed the newspaper covering the top. I will want to read it later. Then I began to lift out first one, a child's sweater, then another, then a couple larger sweaters. There were six in all. A couple men size shirts, a ladies dress and some socks for each of us. Tucked in between was a hat, just for me. Then I found it. A letter neatly folded in my dress. This was the most precious gift of all.

It told of their life and how much she missed me. There was not one word of how she found me. As I read bits and pieces of her letter to the others, I saved some for me to read tomorrow when I would be alone. With a guilty heart, I felt relieved that no one else, especially Floyd, was able to read my long awaited letter. This just may be the help I will need.

She told of how plans were being made for my brother Klaus and two of Floyds cousins to visit in a year from this coming September. A year? How will I ever wait so long. Dear Ursula, had even enclosed a blank piece of paper in an envelope addressed to her, fully stamped. I will write small so I can tell her of my plans. She will understand.

I threw myself into my work with a much

lighter heart. My enthusiasm was greater than it had been for a long time.

Then I began to think of Beulah and George and their marriage. We were not able to attend their ceremony as it was in Prairie Range, but the ladies in our community put on a lovely tea in the Little School House for her. What a fun time we all had reminiscing of her time with us. She told of how they would live on the family farm in their own small house. She already had a position with the Prairie Range school district. The school was a mile and a half from the farm. Her new father-in-law has a horse and small buggy just for her. Their hired hand's wife would help her out in the house as well as help Helen. She was excited and we were happy for her.

Finally it was time to return to our chores and so a final farewell was extended full of hugs and tears. I knew that I would see her one more time before she left easing the sadness for both Katrin and I. Perhaps this was just stretching it out.

In just a few weeks it will be time for the new schoolteacher to arrive. Gary Jenkins is a single man in his early thirties with a frail build and bright red hair, wanting to see the north. All he knew was that it was a one-room schoolhouse with about twenty students in the country. It seems he did not ask and so no one told him the country was nine miles from the nearest small town. He will come with no horse or other means of transportation, and certainly no cooking skills. Was this really what he was looking for?

He already knew how to split wood, start a fire in the cast iron cook stove, but the coal oil lamp and kerosene lanterns were knew to him. He would need to be a quick student. Floyd offered to show Gary when he arrived. Someone from the school board would make arrangements to meet him at the train, and then give him a ride to what was to be his new home for the next two years at least.

Chapter Twenty-Nine

It was nearing the middle of July that the Faust family came to visit bringing with them some poppy seed buns Bertha had baked just that morning for us to enjoy together. As soon as the children had gone outside to climb trees, they told of their plans to go to Reuben to visit with relatives. Johnny could look after their animals but they knew Floyd would need to remain behind to care for ours. She also knew my sister Rose lived in Reuben. We could all travel in their truck with the four kids riding in the back in the closed-in box. As Floyd stressed that we did not have extra money to be spent, how would we manage to eat until we got to Reuben. I too wondered just how I could manage this trip. With not having had time to think this through, my excitement quickly faded. This did not seem possible.

Bertha was ready. She knew how much I needed to see my sister. Bertha had thought this through. She quickly explained that we both had canned chicken and homemade sausage to take along to go with our bread that we would carefully wrap in cloth. We had lots of water too. She would write her cousin Harriett to be in touch with Rose. I would see my fun loving brother Klaus as well.

As Marvin and Floyd wandered the farm checking out the fields, Marvin carefully convinced Floyd that we should go feeling bad that he was not able to come along. After a while it was decided that we should go. Floyd agreed it would be an op-

portunity for me to visit with my sister. Not a word
was to be said to any of the children until the day
before. Bertha quietly gave me a washed flour sack
to make a dress for Katrin. Even some light green
dye to make it pretty as well cover any remaining
spots of red dye left behind. Fritz and I would be
fine with the clothes we had but Katrin could not
go in her brother's old hand-me-down overalls she
wore each day.

We would only be in Reuben for three days,
just enough time for a visit with Rose and her children. Her husband had left her for a younger woman he had met in the pool hall. Now she was doing
housework to earn money to feed and clothe the
four of them. She was left with the small bungalow
house in exchange for his freedom to move in with
his 'dance hall girl'. Each month he agreed to give
her some money to help with the expenses. Much
too often he would forget or need to spend it on
playing pool. If she sent one of her children to collect there was a better chance of him giving something. Seldom what was agreed upon, but even a
little helped.

Rose had two daughters and one son. While
there she gathered together some clothes they had
outgrown but would do nicely for my two. Now Katrin would have a coat and Fritz a suit for church.
While Klaus took us around town to show us the
sights, they so proudly wore their new clothes.
Each moment of each day was full of wonderment
for each of us.

We drank Coca Cola at their factory, ate ice

cream cones from the best soda fountain in Reuben. Their floats with root beer over vanilla ice cream were Fritz's favourite. Cream soda over strawberry ice cream was Katrin's first and only choice. She liked everything pink, including the popcorn that came in little cardboard satchels. There were so many treats for us I really could not choose, I loved them all savouring the delicious flavours.

I drank coffee that someone else had made just for me served with a cookie. This was a dream holiday, one that I could never have imagined. We each thanked Klaus over and over for his generosity. Klaus beamed with love and pride as the children hung on to him as they bounced with excitement enjoying each minute with a real Uncle. This was a love they had never known. For me, it added to my special time with my family I had not seen for so long. I had missed them so much.

The streets were not dusty from the prairie winds blowing sand around, or dirty from the horses having left their mess behind. Cars were parked on both sides of the road leaving me with a dream of owning one of my own someday in my future. Maybe I would be able to have a shiny red one. I wondered why these were all black, red would be nicer. There were streetcars to ride on taking their happy passengers from one end of town to the other, then returning for them at the end of their day. This was a fairy tale place filled with sweets, love and laughter.

In the evenings while Rose and I sat alone at the kitchen table, I shared with her my life. The good and the bad. All of it. Only too often I could see the tears rolling down her cheeks. When Klaus would join us, he too was finding it difficult to accept that this was our life. He assured me that when he came next year he would come with help for my children and I. Yes, they both said we must leave the north. First I must convince Floyd.

As I emptied my heart of how I loved Floyd and did not want to leave him, my tears would not stop flowing. To me he was still the handsome young man of yesterday. They agreed that it was not too likely he would move on. The man they remembered was one of a mild nature, easy to give in to what he had. Not one to take another big chance on what may lie ahead. After demanding her husband leave their house, Rose knew only too well what a mother had to do for her children.

Rose and Klaus both assured me over and over that they would give it much thought. When Klaus and Floyd's cousins come to visit they would speak to us both of any possibilities they could find in the meantime. There had to be a way out. They too feared the hard life in the north might be too much. So many people have succumbed to it already. Where are the rich farmers they had heard so much of? Not in the cold windy north.

After a tearful goodbye we headed north again, but this time in a pickup truck. As we bounced along over the rough roads I spent the first while thinking of our time in Reuben. Running water, electricity, an indoor bathroom and a telephone. I was so happy for Rose for these conveniences. I knew she too worked long and hard each day cleaning houses to provide for her children and their schooling. Sometimes she brought some laundry home with her as she rode on the streetcar to earn a little extra.

As we travelled along we could hear Fritz and Katrin repeating a cute little rhyme their older cousins had taught them.

> *It's raining,*
> *It's pouring,*
> *The old man is snoring,*
> *So jump in bed,*
> *Cover your head,*
> *And don't get up until morning.*

Soon Carmen and Grace were joining in as they chanted away.

All too soon we were home again on our farm into the same routine of chores and sleep. By now the weeds in the garden had taken a life of their own, they were everywhere. The summer sunshine had given them a boost of energy. With the extra help from Katrin and Fritz we had most of them pulled out within a few long days. While they pulled out the larger weeds, I hoed under the smaller ones all the while with my mind on Reuben. We could not let them rob our garden of its nutrients.

I now began to prepare for butchering day, for a day of soap making and preparing the cellar for the fall canning. Each day was bringing the cool fall days that much closer. The garden vegetables would need to be picked and canned before the fall frost had a chance to cast its' nasty spell on our food supply. The winter coats and boots would need to be checked for any mending needing to be done should we wake to a sudden snow storm while we had slept.

One late summer afternoon I was in the garden picking vegetables that were ready to eat and can when I heard the sound of an Indian wagon on the road. Their wagons had a distinct sound that I grew up to recognize. I let go of my apron dropping the freshly picked rhubarb onto the ground and raced to the road in hopes of seeing Mary. By the time I ran through the trees taking the short cut, all I was able to see was the back of a wagon. An Indian wagon. I called out as loud as I could but no one heard me. As I slowly walked back to the garden I thought of how I had come to hide when I heard an Indian wagon to wishing with all my heart they were coming to visit me. I had come to love the sound of their ponies as they trotted along the road pulling their creaky wagons, unlike our heavy workhorses.

Later that evening as Floyd and I sat at the table discussing our day's work, I brought up the subject of the Indian wagon travelling past our farm. I was so disappointed to learn that he had not heard them. He had been working on the east side of our land, which meant there was no way for him to see the road. I knew by the look on his face that he was as disappointed as I was.

By the time we decided it was time to call it the end to a very long day, we decided to go to town on Saturday. If necessary I would spend the entire afternoon at the General Store while Floyd would spend his time near the livery stable. He had wanted to have a short visit with Jimmy, the local Blacksmith. With Jimmy's shop being in the same area it was often a gathering place for men. As much as we felt we had been careful to speak of this only after the children had gone to sleep, Fritz had already said he would tell us if he should see their tribe in town.

Chapter Thirty

The first day of school began with much excitement from all the students. They had seen very little of their friends during the summer, some not at all. Then there was the new teacher. Someone from the school board would attend for a short while on the first morning to remind students of the rules they needed to obey. A reminder that Mr. Jenkins was to be respected at all times. This brought a couple smart-alecky remarks from a couple insolent students just loud enough to be heard but not understood by the new teacher. He did now know who the difficult students and their followers were. He just knew he had his work cut out for him, but he would win. It would be just a typical first day on the job.

By lunchtime on the first day these same students were mimicking the way their teacher walked. At six years of age he had been helping his father in the field with the raking when he tripped and fell into the path of the rake. As it ran over his left leg his pant leg became caught preventing him from pulling himself free. Feeling forever grateful that he did not loose his leg, he was left with a permanent limp. He had grown accustomed to being teased at the beginning of each new group of students that were getting to know him. They would soon learn their lessons. It would not take long until they would see who was in charge. It would take time.

A couple weeks after school began, I received

another note in Fritz`s lunch pail that nurse Miss Opal would visit the following week on Tuesday. Would I be available to help? Floyd and I were both excited for this day to come. It would give me an opportunity to check on how things were going between the new teacher and his students.

I intentionally arrived a few minutes early. As I waited in the cloakroom I was able to observe the classroom at the same time. The cloakroom was neat, tidy and clean. I was in awe as to the orderly way the students behaved. They raised their hands before speaking. The older unruly students politely called him Mr. Jenkins. There were no flying objects propelled through the air, no dipping of the girl's hair into their inkwells as they listened to the teacher with last minute instructions for Miss Opal's arrival. I was impressed. How did he manage this in such a short time? Perhaps their new behaviour was for my benefit.

Soon Miss Opal arrived and I went into the classroom. When Miss Opal and I entered the classroom, Mr. Jenkins nodded his head and then in unison the students wearing their everyday farm clothes said hello ladies. Imagine that. Was this teacher a miracle worker? Tonight we will have much to discuss at the dinner table.

When I had Mr. Jenkin's desk ready, he instructed the students to line up on the right side of the room. There was no pushing or shoving. Jake, the oldest and biggest boy did not pick up a smaller student swinging him or her back and forth or over his head loudly saying 'go wee wee' as he had been known to do in the past. To his delight, this had been sure to bring much disruption to the class.

A while later, as I walked to the door with Miss Opal, she motioned for me to step outside with her. With a most bewildered look on her face, she asked, "What happened? I have never seen those two so well behaved either here or in town."

I assured her I knew nothing about it but hoped to find out before someone from Cross Cut came to visit in case he had done something to get himself in trouble. Just what it could be, I did not know.

As we ate our dinner that evening I brought up the subject of Mr. Jenkins. I began by speaking of Miss Opal and her visit drawing both Fritz and Katrin into the conversation hoping they would extend the conversation to Mr. Jenkins. Not a chance. They were not making it easy for me so I decided to just come straight out and ask.

I began by complimenting the students on how nice the cloakroom looked.

"So who cleans and tidies it up?" I asked.

"We all do" they said speaking in unison as they so often did. "We all have to stay until its clean just the way Mr. Jenkins likes it," said Katrin.

We spoke of the appearance both inside and outside of the school for the next few minutes. They told what the new rules were. They never mentioned of any consequences should anyone not comply so I left the subject be. They seemed to be excited about the new schoolyard games they were learning during lunch and recess. Everyone could take part, even Clay.

Now it was Floyd's turn to ask questions regarding the older boys that always seemed to disrupt the class each year. All they knew was that Mr. Jenkins had visited their farms to speak with their parents. Fritz told of how they are polite and obedient, even helping the teacher and other students. Katrin quietly said they are even learning to read in their Dick and Jane readers. Now we both knew that something good was going to come with this new teacher. Perhaps being a little older man is the answer.

When Sunday afternoon came, I sent the children to the Little School House to invite Mr. Jenkins over for supper. After a while I saw the three of them walking along the road stopping every once in a while to look at some wild flowers. I knew they were both happy to show off their knowledge of the local wildflowers and berries. This gave them an opportunity to get to know their teacher a little better.

As they entered the house all three were full of smiles with the appearance of being most comfortable with each other. It seems Mr. Jenkins had won the hearts of his students rather quickly.

After supper the men went outside to look over the fields and the barnyard as well as get acquainted a little more. After a short while Mr. Jenkins thanked us for supper and headed home. He wanted to prepare some work for the older students for the next day before retiring.

As Fritz and Katrin prepared for bed I knew this was my chance to get their feelings on their teacher. They both readily said they really liked him. Then Katrin asked me why his mouth always smells funny. Immediately I am on high alert. I would need to carefully and slowly question them over the next short while.

Later that evening as Floyd and I sat at the table before turning the lamp out for the night, I mentioned what our children had said. He said he had picked up on something that Mr. Jenkins had said in passing. Perhaps the first Saturday we can we will go to town inviting Mr. Jenkins to come along. Without being offensive, we will try to be aware of how much alcohol he purchases. This too will give us an opportunity to check on any new Indian Tribes arriving.

A week later the weather was sunny and clear with little wind. We decided this was the day for town. When the chores were complete, I began heating the bath water for the family. It was now too cool to put the tub outside in front of the house so until next summer bathing would be inside. First Katrin as she was the cleanest, giving me time to brush and braid her long curly hair while Fritz bathed. My turn was next and then Floyd. He never minded that the water was not fresh and hot. By now the towel was very damp too, actually wet. For me I found being able to have the tub outside was much easier to empty leaving no water on the linoleum floor. As Fritz and Katrin were now off to extend our invitation to Mr. Jenkins, we spoke of our concerns and how we were going to handle them.

As we neared the outskirts of Weesp, Floyd steered the team to the South Road. Immediately Fritz questioned him. This was not our usual way into town but it would take us past the reservation. Floyd calmly said that he thought it would be a good day to show Mr. Jenkins the South side of town.

As we slowly trotted along we pointed out several of the farms and who lived there. Fritz was the first one to spot the teepees on the Reservation. Giving Katrin a quick look and then me, I knew he had heard at least some of one of our conversations. I slowly shook my head sideways and then said a prayer that he would not tell Katrin, at least not until we get home. That would be the most I could hope for. Now we would need to figure out our next step.

A teepee is an Indian tent made from animal skins laid on a conical frame of long poles. The buffalo skin was stretched over the skeleton of poles. They were tied together near the top leaving a hole for the smoke to escape. The flap at the bottom served as a doorway. It is warm in the winter, cool in the summer and could withstand all kinds of weather. They were also easy to move. As there were a few of them standing to the far side, we would need to be sure we were welcome before going onto their land.

As we drove through town on our way to the livery stable, Floyd and I noticed an Indian Chief in full headdress and his family wearing their buckskin clothes sitting on the sidewalk outside the general store. I was so excited I nearly jumped out of the wagon. As we past a couple more stores Floyd pulled the team to a stop. He calmly suggested I get out there giving me more time to visit. He firmly said the rest could go with him. While Fritz whined a little, he knew not to push it or he would be staying in the wagon a while longer.

As I neared the front of the store, Bertha came hurrying out exclaiming "Emma, how nice to see you today!" She stopped me on the sidewalk making it obvious to me that we would chat out there. My heart was beating so loud I could hardly hear myself think of my next step.

"Hello Bertha. Floyd dropped me off a little closer today so I would not have so far to walk," I replied trying to sound calm while being sure I could be heard just in case Mary was with them.

I was sure that I could see an Indian mother about my age with two children around the age of mine. I could not look for more than a couple seconds without being rude.

While Bertha and I exchanged greetings, I tried to discreetly get a few glimpses of this mother. With my left hand I pushed my hair back a few times, a habit I had since my teenage years hoping Mary would recognize it.

In a couple short minutes the Chief came out of the store promptly followed with his tribe standing. As they turned to leave I felt someone looking at me. As I dared to look over she turned and with her head lowered walked away. To my memory Mary frequently walked with her head lowered slightly. As though I was the only one around my eyes followed them down the street. As they turned onto the South Road she looked over her shoulder holding her gaze on me for a few seconds. This had to be Mary.

Before Bertha and I parted company she suggested that we visit them soon. Today she had purchased everything needed to make Root Beer. As we had discussed previously with the men, when the rodeo came to town we would all go. However, we would watch from the grassy bank so as to not have to pay an entrance fee or a fee for leaving the horses in the corral. We would take a lunch with us. There would be enough time for the yeast concoction to ferment and do its work. This would be a great and special treat as well as fun to make.

Chapter Thirty-One

As Floyd walked through town he noticed Gary Jenkins talking to a couple men around his age outside the drug store. As they were dressed farm style, overalls with a plaid shirt and a hat, he wondered what had drawn them together. One a teacher, the other a farmer. When he got close to them, Gary stopped him to introduce him to his new friends. Floyd was not familiar with their families as they came from a community south of Weesp, but he was happy to see that he had found some men his own age to visit with.

As he neared the Elevators he met up with Marvin as he was returning from his stop at the post office. Each time he went to town he stopped in to see if just by chance someone had been inquiring of Johnny. Again it was no, there is nothing. This was the same answer he had received for the past few years but was not willing to give up. There must be someone missing this shy young man.

As they slowly walked on Floyd asked if he too had seen the Tribe outside the General Store. Shaking his head he explained that all he had seen was their wagon at the end of town partly hidden amongst a cluster of Birch trees. For the next while they shared ideas as they walked around the edges of town. It seemed there was no easy answer. They both agreed that if Mary were with them, I would have seen her.

As Floyd and I visited with other people we had come to know, the main topic of concern seemed to be the other farm boy that had not as yet returned to his family. It was agreed by all that he would not have gone to the northern community as it was even more desolate than the Weesp area. There surely would be no extra work on their farms to be done, nor could they afford to feed one more mouth. The plan that was left was for all to inquire with those we might meet in our travels. Could he have been as fortunate as Johnny to find his way to a farmer willing and able to help him? No one would even think of making him return to his family where they had too many children to care for. Just to be sure he was warm and fed.

Much too soon it was time to have Fritz and Katrin find Gary to meet us at our wagon near the livery stable. As we climbed in neither Floyd or I noticed him carrying anything other than a small bag from the General Store. This would be sure to include some coffee, tobacco, cigarette papers and likely some bread and cookies.

As we headed out of town, Floyd once again took the South Road. As we went by the Reservation, Gary made comment on the Indians in town. His interest in them was much different from ours. He thought of the Reservation as ways to educate his students. Perhaps they would understand their way of living if they were able to observe first-hand. Most importantly, they would treat them with more respect verbally as they learned of their ways. I thought this would be a good idea but just how was he going to do that. Before he carried out this plan, he would need to discuss it with the school board.

I tried to keep my eyes open for any sign of anyone moving around. Both Floyd and I noticed a few children running around as a fire was being started, probably in preparation for their evening meal. There still was no sign of Mary.

Later that evening as Floyd and I sat at the table we spoke of how and when we could visit the Reservation. If anyone could be trusted by their Chief I felt sure it would be Floyd. With his slow but steady walk, his presence would not be one of concern. He had spoke with many of the Chiefs in town but only for a minute to greet them assuring them he meant no harm. Now we wondered what the reaction would be when on their land, and un-invited.

We both felt that we must do this soon just in case something was to frighten them away. They had been known to be there in the evening, but when morning came there would be no trace of them. They would leave before daylight, not hav-ing made a sound. The wind and dust removed even the slightest trace of their visit.

The next morning Floyd had already gone out to begin chores before I had the fire in the cook stove heated up. If I did not hurry he would be coming in for breakfast before I began my milking. Even when the weather was not good, I seemed to find relaxation in this time. As I leaned my fore-head against Bossy, I knew I could talk to her. She always listened.

As always the day seemed to go by quickly. I

would hardly get my morning chores finished when it would be time to take lunch to Floyd if he was in the field. Today was one of those days. This did give us a couple minutes to discuss the options we had both thought of. There seemed to be only one realistic option. Yes, next week we will do it.

We still needed to discuss the concern of Gary but this would need to wait until later. It did not seem as though there was any big problem but we shall not dismiss it without making sure first. He was such a good teacher we did not want to see him doing anything to tarnish his image.

Friday came with the weather promising to be another great day ahead. Tomorrow we would go to town again. This was certainly not usual. There was too much work to be done particularly at this time of year. We worked extra hard doing as much extra as possible. Again, we would invite Gary along.

Morning came with my not having slept much during the long night. For the first few hours I was cold, then my back hurt from the extra work. I knew the biggest problem was that I was so worried as to how this day would go. I could not relax. Would Mary be able to speak to me if she was there? My mind was whirling and whirling with the many possibilities that were likely to never happen. I wondered how I would deal with the ones that did.

Finally it was time to send word to Gary that he was invited to town again. When he arrived with a puzzled look on his face, he thanked us for the opportunity to perhaps spend some time talking with his friends again. As we climbed into the wagon, Fritz asked if we were going to look for the Indians again. Katrin wanted to know if she could talk to their children. Now that was a surprise from a girl who was too shy to speak to our neighbours. Whatever was she thinking? Afraid that they would ask further questions in town, I gave them my mother look that said this was adult talk, not to be discussed now. While I knew that Fritz was doing as told, it would not be for long.

This time Floyd did not take the Westgate Road to South Road. He thought it best that we stay with our regular route. As we entered the farm on the muskeg hoping to take a short cut, the gate was closed. Even though it just leaned against the post that was as good as being locked. Just as we thought we would have to back the team and wagon up to turn around, one of the older boys came welcoming us to travel on their land opening the gate for us. With many thanks, we proceeded through taking heed of his warning of the wet and muddy path ahead.

Just as we were nearing the other side we saw what Floyd dreaded to see. He would need to get out and lead the team through. The mud was deep and very soft. It held all the signs of earlier wagons having been stuck in this slick muck. Before climbing out of the wagon, he put on his gum boots that he had always put in the wagon just in case. This was for sure one of those times.

Holding on to Buck's bridle, Floyd ever so

slowly led our team through this treacherous path all the while holding his breath neither Buck or Misty would slip and fall. As though they too knew the dangers, they each patiently placed one foot carefully down before lifting the other. It seemed it took a very long time before our wagon was safely on solid ground again where we could all breathe with ease. We knew we had taken an enormous risk.

The remainder of the way to town, we travelled in relative silence, slowing down only long enough to greet other travellers as we met. I had always noticed that regardless of their language, there would be a friendly greeting with a warm smile. Today was no different.

As we reached the outskirts of town, Floyd then headed for South Road taking us past the Red and White Store. Travelling slowly, we both scanned the sides of the buildings as well as the treed areas for any sign of their ponies or wagon. We saw none.

When I arrived at the General Store I found only Mr. Bosch there. The store was void of customers. We began a friendly conversation concerning the weather followed by the roads from our farm into town. Soon while there was just him and I, he asked me if there was a particular connection or concern with the Indian Tribe. As he noticed my hesitation, he placed his hand on my arm like the tender older gentleman he was.

"Is this matter a personal one?" he asked. "Your story will be safe with me. Perhaps I can help."

Mr. Bosch was a gentleman that I had liked from my first day in town. He always had a friendly smile and a warm greeting pertaining to just me. I had come to trust him completely. His gentle nature gave me such comfort I wanted to pour my heart out. I missed my father so much; it was easy to fall in love with this compassionate sweet man.

I wanted to tell him of my friend Mary, how I promised her mother to keep a watchful eye for her but at the same time keeping her secret. As I looked into his tender green eyes I nodded in agreement fearing that if I spoke my tears would fall. I felt his arm resting on my shoulders as he began to tell me of this tribe that comes north every spring staying until fall.

Mr. Bosch told me that Chief Barefoot and his people first visited Weesp a few years ago for one season only. He spoke with him very briefly each time they came for supplies. He went on to say that he found Chief Barefoot to be a quiet man speaking only as needed in his limited English. At the end of the season, he and his tribe moved on not returning until last spring. Mr. Bosch understood from the druggist that they had been visiting Prairie Range General store, as there was a Reservation nearby unoccupied.

As I became more and more comfortable, I began to relate pieces of my story of Mary and her parents. Asking me few questions, listening patiently, he assured me he understood my concern and that I must take advantage of each moment before it is too late.

He went on to say that he had not noticed a white lady about my age with them as only the Chief comes into the store. With an assurance that I felt was sincere, he would do all he could to see if Mary is with them. By now he had become friendly with Chief Barefoot and so felt comfortable to ask. He would try to determine when they would be in town again. Most farmers had a routine, as did they.

For some unusual reason, his store remained mostly free of other customers and so we began to talk freely. He asked me where we came from and how we got there. I tried to explain why we felt we had to leave Estuary for the north. As we spoke he occasionally excused himself to wait upon a customer hurrying back to ask more questions.

When Floyd came in looking for me I quickly explained how Mr. Bosch knew our reason for being in town. By now it was most likely too late in the day for them to visit so we may as well leave. Mr. Bosch said he was not too comfortable with the idea of Floyd entering their Reservation. Please give me an opportunity to speak with Chief Barefoot so as to not upset their people giving them cause to be afraid, he requested. Floyd agreed that this was probably the best way for now.

Soon we were on our way home. As soon as we turned off Main Street onto North Road both Buck and Misty picked up their pace. Floyd would need to keep a tight hold on the reins. They knew they were going home, and home meant to their stall in the barn. There would be soft hay with its sweet smell waiting for them. Dinner always came soon after. Their harnesses would be removed, their thick dark coats would be brushed making their backs feel light and clean. Their foreheads would be scratched with soft-spoken words in their ear. They knew they had done a good job.

A few days later we received word from Mr. Bosch via Cecil Swain that we should come to town on Wednesday afternoon. Cecil had no idea what it was about other than he had a message for us. After a short visit Cecil said it was time to head home. He had been away from his chores too long already. We both thanked him for his time and trouble assuring him all was well with our family.

On Sunday afternoon we walked to the Little School House to speak to Gary. Perhaps he would come home with Fritz and Katrin after the other students had gone home as we did not know how long we might be. Leaving Fritz and Katrin to play in the schoolyard, we were able to speak privately with Gary. He assured us it was no problem. He would help them begin chores. Now what does a city boy know about milking and feeding cows? We would leave instructions with Fritz as to what all they needed to do. Katrin would need to prepare their supper. She was already able to use the stove. Fritz would need to light the fire for her as soon as they came home.

The next day, I prepared pork stew in the morning for their supper using potatoes, onions and carrots from our garden. Katrin could heat it up, set the table, and cut some bread for them. They would be fine.

As soon as we had our noonday meal of stew, we set off for town. On our past trips, I filled most of the time admiring the green trees and wild grasses, especially the soft fluffy wild fox tails showing their golden colour with wild flowers growing nearby. Most of the flowers were delicate with a rich colour unique to each. Today it was Floyd pointing out the things to see as we made our way to town. I knew he felt I needed a little help to pass the time.

Finally we reached the field near the livery stable. There we would leave our team to rest until we were ready for the return trip. There was no charge for the use of this pasture unlike the livery stable. Floyd would leave feed for them to munch on as well as grass while they patiently waited.

I was sure I had walked slowly to the General Store but Floyd, with a chuckle in his voice, said I ran slowly. Whichever, I could not wait to get there.

Once inside I found Mr. Bosch busy helping a gentleman choosing some tools near the back of the store. I browsed around so as to not make either of them feel hurried. How I wished I could just say, please just take something so you can leave. With no sight of anyone special outside I began to wonder just what was about to happen, if anything.

Soon Floyd was at my side quietly whispering in my ear that he was sure he heard the ponies on South Road. Now I became so nervous I did not hear Mr. Bosh ask to speak to us in the hardware area. When Floyd took my hand and began to tug me to follow him, I suddenly felt faint; my knees were turning to rubber. Within a few seconds I collapsed onto the floor. A minute later I heard some chanting as I regained consciousness. I could not understand what Floyd was saying or why he would be speaking so differently to me.

Then a canteen of water was in front of me with drops of cool water seeping into my lips. I felt the warmth of a soft gentle hand on my forehead. Was it my name I heard over and over as darkness took over once again?

Later Floyd relayed to me the events of the previous hour. He told of how they were not able to bring me around with water so he ran across the street to the Drug Store shouting all the way for the druggist to come with the smelling salts.

Mr. Durham was an older gentleman just waiting to retire in one more year. With his snow-white hair and portly stature, one could see why he said he was not able to run. By the time he hurried to his locked cabinet, removed the salts, and then made his way across the road to the General Store still wearing his white druggist jacket, he himself was puffing as he struggled to get his breath.

As Floyd took the salts and held it beneath my nose to breath in, I quickly came around. Now it was Mr. Bosch who was assisting Mr. Durham with a few sips of water as a customer held a wet cloth to his forehead. It was a few more minutes before he realized that he had left his store unattended. Mr. Bosch quickly assured him that he had asked one of his customers to tend to his store for a short while. There is no need to worry of his honesty; he has looked after my store many times for me over the past few years. He is as honest as the day is long, explained Mr. Bosch.

It was about an hour before life began to return to normal in this popular store. I was still feeling embarrassed with all the fussing over me. Dear sweet Mr. Bosch said I was just too tired to cope with all the anticipation of my lost friend possibly coming to town.

As soon as Floyd and I were alone, I asked him if it was ponies I thought I had heard. Knowing immediately what I meant, he assured me it was but was too busy to see where they had fled. I tried my best to be strong so as to not show my disappointment at having missed my chance to see my friend.

After thanking Mr. Bosch for his help, we made arrangements as to when we felt we would once again come to town. Perhaps Chief Barefoot and his people would come once more. Mr. Bosch would ask.

As we slowly began to leave town Floyd turned the wagon around to head for the South Road and then we could take the Farm Road north. This would take us an extra hour at least but it may be a fruitful drive.

As we neared the road leading into our farm, we could see Gary, Fritz and Katrin beside the road. Trying not to think of bad things having happened, we both wondered what this was about. When we reached them we knew. They had Boxer, our Boxer dog, in the ditch frantically washing him with some lye soap as they each turned their heads away every couple minutes to catch a breath of fresh air. They didn't need to explain that Boxer had met up with a skunk that was likely wandering around near the barn. His now unpleasant pungent odour was making their eyes water and Katrin's stomach turn so much that she was gagging.

By now all three were wet up to their knees. This large black dog with his large floppy ears, droopy cheeks and nose that looked like it was made from rubber, stood there with the most mournful look I have ever seen him display. They had been moving along the ditch as they washed him to find fresh water, still to no avail.

When Floyd suggested they have done all they could, they may as well leave him to dry off. They should each go in and change into some clothes that smelled better. He will just have to depend on the outdoor air and time to relieve him of this nasty smell.

After thanking Gary for all his help as we began to laugh at the sight of them, he turned with a wave and headed north to his home beside the Little School House. I reminded everyone that there was absolutely no way that Boxer could come inside the house while he smelled like a skunk and not a dog. He will need to sleep in the barn until then. Even the sad look in his eyes did not help to change my mind.

With a reminder to the children to not leave their clothes in the house, they both took off in a run just too eager to get rid of that awful smell. They both knew they would have to wash at the well tonight.

Chapter Thirty-Two

Life on our farm was a busy life. It seemed not much changed from day to day. There were chores and more chores. Every once-in-a-while something would happen to cause us concern. Today it was Belle. She seemed to be listless. As she was the one to lead the herd to greener pastures they were all standing around the coral looking forlorn. Floyd began to give her extra care and attention coaxing her to eat. He mixed a special mixture containing small pieces of potato to encourage her to want to eat. It was impossible to send word to town for a vet to visit. Floyd would once again have to use his experience that he had learned along life's way. We could not possibly afford the extra expense nor could we afford to loose one of our precious cows. This was a farmer's nightmare.

That night Floyd made his bed in a pile of hay next to Belle's stall. He wanted to be there in case she cried for help. When morning came I went to the barn to see how things were. Belle was sound asleep in her stall while Floyd had begun his chores. Since he had not been able to sleep more than a few winks at a time he thought he might as well get started. Perhaps after the noon meal he may be able to stretch out for a few minutes.

I soon hurried back to the house to get breakfast ready for the family. I would try to help out with doing some extra chores today. When the morning meal was prepared I went to the barn to relieve Floyd for watch duty so he could go inside for some hot porridge and coffee.

As I sat on the soft hay beside Belle stroking her neck, she lay quietly giving me a soft moo every while especially when I stopped stroking her soft hair. I think she just needed a little extra rest and attention. Floyd agreed. For the remainder of the day we let her stay in her stall for some quiet time. When I milked her later in the day she willingly gave what she had even though it was not her usual amount.

Once again Floyd slept in the barn so as to be nearby should she be in distress during the night. When morning came Belle rose with the rest of the herd, ready and eager to be fed and watered. After milking she joined the others as they meandered out to the pasture to graze as they too enjoyed the beauty and warmth of sunshine. Much to our relief she appeared to be her old self.

After the noon meal, Floyd lay on the bed for a short rest while I cleared the dishes. Then I prepared as much as I could for supper so I too could have a rest. Like Belle I had not been feeling too well. My energy seemed to have vanished. While we had no medicine other than Watkins Medicated Ointment, we both felt the best medicine for us was to take the time for some extra rest. Sometimes we found that hard to do since there was so much work to be done. We had both learned from our parents that rest was the best rather than wait until we were too run down.

This coming Sunday afternoon there was to be a Social at the Little School House. While I was anxious to see the other Ladies for some social time, Floyd was wishing for a ball game. Those men were like a group of schoolboys when they got together. What with their kibitzing with each other, laughing and cheering their worries of the farms were left behind for a while. Invariably during the game one of the men would switch a dried cow pie for a soft one waiting to see whose misfortune it would be this time.

Sunday afternoon came with the skies shinning clear and bright. The early fall breeze held a touch of a feel for an early night's frost soon to come. I silently prayed that it would not be for a while yet as we were not ready. To be ready all the harvesting needed to be complete. I knew this Social was to build the spirits of the farmers for the tough work ahead. There would be no time for another Social for a while.

The next while we spent working extra hard making each day last as long as possible to beat the winter storms. Soon the first snow of the season will begin to fall. I know that it will be any day now.

Just as I thought, one afternoon while in the house checking to see if the bread has risen enough to bake. I checked the oven heat by putting my hand inside for a second to test the temperature. Feeling that it was now ready, I carefully placed the pans in the oven. Until it was baked to a nice golden brown, I kept a close eye on the fire as it burnt. In order to keep an even temperature, the wood had to be steady with just the right amount of coals glowing a beautiful red. Now I would heat some lard in my deep fry pan to make a fried bread treat. I stood still as in a dream remembering my days as a young girl enjoying this treat.

I looked out the window to see softly falling large flakes of sparkly white snow coming from the heavens ever so gently. Soon our farm would be a white blanket of freshness. The first early fall made one feel so full of peace and wonderment. In a couple hours it would be a wonder to behold. The trees would wear a thin white coat sparkling in the sunshine. The wood fences took on a look of white wash, so clean and fresh. By evening we would be able to hear the crunch of the crisp snow under our boots as we walked around our white farm seeing only a white sky. The stars were hiding. After a couple minutes I began to wonder how long it would be this year before the fence posts could no longer be seen as they hid waiting for spring thaw and the warm sunshine.

Later that evening as I was walking to the house I began to think of where the years have gone since we left Estuary. In a couple more months we will see the end of 1945. We were just as poor as when we arrived in the north. My children were nearing the end of their educational years. I had promised myself I would do better for them. Where did I fail? I knew I was no closer to leaving the north for a better life for my family.

I could find no fault with Floyd for our meagre life. He too had worked long and hard each day loving his children more than himself. His only fault would be that he was satisfied to spend the remainder of our years like this. I knew he too prayed that God would take care of us. He was taking care of us, but could He not have found a little extra for us to reward our children for our struggles. I desperately wanted a better life, not a richer life, just an easier life. I wondered if we were ready to crumble at this young age, how would we cope as we became older. Would we live to be older?

Later that evening after Fritz and Katrin had fallen asleep, I sat at the table with the dim light of our lamp flickering as it burned. Today I should have cleaned the smoke from the glass chimney so as to give off a brighter light. I listened to the crackle of the wood in the cook stove snapping as it left behind a red glow breaking into smaller pieces. More than ever, this night I wished I had a soft comfortable chair to rest my tired sore back as the tears rolled down my cheeks. My dreams were shattered. I was no closer to finding Mary or to a better life.

Chapter Thirty-Three

Much to my relief we had survived this past winter, how I do not know. I continued to send my children to school most every day even though some days it was snowing fiercely with the winds driving the cold into their faces. Most days it would be around forty below but still we struggled forward.

When so many in the community had suffered hardships of a different kind, I tried to be mindful of my family not having any accidents or sickness that a little Watkins Medicated Ointment rolled into a ball of sugar and swallowed could not fix.

This spring I was to find that we were not as fortunate as I had thought. While out in the field helping Floyd in the early spring, I tripped over a root from a stray willow tree wanting to branch out on its own. Over I went falling into the cold dirt wondering what had just happened. When I tried to stand I knew. I had twisted my left ankle. I could not stand. I had no choice but to wait for Floyd to come looking for me. I knew it would be soon.

After getting me settled in the house, he went to the well for some ice cold water to soak my ankle in hopes it would keep the swelling at bay. After cutting a branch from a tree for me to lean on, we were both back to our chores. I was just much slower. Now the family had to help me carry my share of the load.

It was weeks before I was able to walk without the aid of my stick. This was not the way I wished for others to see me. I felt it would just be another reason to look at us with pity in their eyes. I chose to stay close to the farm letting Floyd and the children make the trip to town for the supplies that could no longer wait.

One mild day as I was scrubbing the floor with the door open, Floyd sent the children in on the run to tell me that we were getting visitors from the City. I could hear them yelling to me all the way from the corral. Immediately I knew who it was. They always seemed to come at the most inopportune time. This time I truly looked like a poor scrub woman. Whatever could I do? I stood there and cried. We would be pitied once again.

As the days passed, I threw myself into my mission of leaving the north, with or without my husband. First I needed to be more aggressive in my search for Mary. I had to try my best to find her just as I had told her mother I would. More than ever I needed to have a visit with my dear friend Bertha. Perhaps a chat with someone that understood my troubles would help to set my heart and mind at ease. I knew what I just had to do.

When Floyd said he could not possibly take the time away from the farm for a few more weeks, I firmly informed him that I would take Misty and our little buggy myself. He knew that I had been driving a team since I was a teenager so he was not worried. I would be back long before dark. When he had been working in the field, I had taken the opportunity to check the condition of the buggy. It would do just fine. Promising to not cut through the muskeg, a couple days later I set out for town.

As I entered the General Store I was relieved to not see any other customers inside. Mr. Bosch was quick to greet me assuring me there was no need to be frightened. He explained how he had spoken to Chief Barefoot of my concern. He felt that the Chief did somewhat understand the main part of the conversation. Chief Barefoot is a man of his word, but very few. Today they would come to town. Now I must wait patiently. We would need to be gentle in our ways so as to not give the impression we are being aggressive.

I had just gone outside to take a walk along the street to get some fresh air and perhaps settle my nerves a little when I saw them walking along Main Street towards the General Store. Suddenly I could not figure out which direction I should go. If I continued towards them, would I frighten them away? Should I turn around and go back to the General Store? I found myself riveted to the road. My feet would not move. My heart would not slow down. I was staring straight ahead. The Chief was walking straight ahead with his eyes on me, his people following close behind. I must step to the side to let him pass but still I could not move.

Suddenly the Chief was directly in front of me, barely inches away. I heard this strange soft voice say Tansi. As I tried my best to breath and smile I extended my hand as I too said Hello. Of course he did not take my hand but rather raised his right hand to his shoulder, palm towards me. I knew that was his way of saying hello. Then he pointed

Doreen Brust Johnson

to the General Store at which time I turned to begin walking back. Much to my surprise I found him
walking beside me. This was totally unheard of.

As we entered the store I realized that I had
not even taken a quick look to see if Mary was
with them. With mostly sign language, Mr. Bosch
seemed to be able to explain what it was I wanted.
After a short while of this strange conversation,
Mr. Bosch nodded to the door and me.

With my stomach in my throat I quickly turned
to head for the door knocking over a stand of galvanized household pails. As I tried to pick them
up, I became all thumbs making more noise than I
already had. Chief Barefoot bent down beside me
to help. Then he pointed to the door. I understood.
My mind was going faster than my feet. I would
not back down now. This was the moment I had
been waiting for.

Chapter Thirty-Four

As I walked out to the sidewalk I felt my legs shake, my stomach was in turmoil. I began to wonder if Mary wanted to be found. Now Emma, no turning back I chided myself.

When I neared her, she stood up. The others remained seated on the dusty rickety sidewalk. In her face I could see no emotion. As I stopped in front of her, I saw water begin to fill her eyes just as it did mine. I knew she remembered. All I could softly stammer was Mary. It is Emma. What seemed like minutes later she nodded as the tears began to gently flow down her beautiful brown face? I did not realize that I too was crying.

After what seemed like hours, I reached toward her hoping for a friendly reaction. I was already aware that these people do not outwardly show signs of affection. When Mary placed her hand in mine, we both felt the familiar touch that we were so accustomed to in our younger years. Then I heard her whisper the sweetest word she could have said. Emma.

For the next few minutes, we both stood holding hands as we gazed into each others tears. Suddenly out of nowhere a handsome man in buckskins stood beside Mary. It was as if he had floated in on a wispy white cloud. I knew it was Achak.

As he raised his right hand in greeting, his left hand on Mary's shoulder, staring into my eyes, I heard his firm but gentle words, "Amitola, my woman!" I returned with a slight nod. I did not know what else to do. I knew he was in charge of Mary, or rather Amitola. She was his woman.

Soon Chief Barefoot returned speaking to his people in a language I could not understand. After a few moments they all turned and walked away leaving Achak and Mary with me.

Clearing his throat to get my attention, Mr. Bosch motioned for us to go into his store leading us to the back room. With Achak following close behind me, Mary walked along keeping her eyes downward. I did not know if this was still her childhood habit or was she afraid of her husband. I would not be afraid of him or his knife. Something inside told me that he would not hurt anyone, especially Mary.

Once inside the back room, Mary opened up to me. Her English was difficult for her to remember, but soon there was chatting and laughter mixed in with our sniffles. Just the way we were as young ladies preparing for our future life. Without uttering a word, his eyes saying it all, Achak looked at Mary, then me, turned and left the room.

As we stood looking deep into each other's eyes, we brushed our tears away. I was so grateful that for some unknown reason I had placed an extra clean hankie in my pocket. It was just the right one for Mary. What had I been thinking? She readily accepted it, clutching it close to her cheeks.

It seemed that neither one knew where to start. First I wanted to be assured that she was happy in her new life. She said she felt that was where she belonged. I wished I could have told her about her heritage but it was not for me to tell. I quickly told her how concerned her parents were for her. Perhaps she could find a way to talk to them. With so much sorrow in her eyes, she said that while she thinks of them each day she has had to promise to put that life behind speaking no more of it. She clearly loved her husband and three children. She could not give them up.

I tried my best to assure her that they were well but carried heavy hearts for their daughter. They are missing you so much, I explained. Please give me a message for them that I could pass on through Klaus when he comes. I miss them was her solemn reply. Nothing more.

For the next few minutes we talked of my children. I was trying to keep this special time light and easy. Then Achak came in. I quickly decided to take a chance and ask them to visit us on our farm, just for a few minutes to meet Floyd and the children. After they exchanged a few words, Mary said yes. This was the first time there was a smile on her face. I began to breath again. Achak nodded to me.

Give me the directions, she said and I will tell Achak. He will remember.

So I said "take the north road out of Weesp. Stay on it until you have gone past the muskeg on the west side. Then take the road that goes west. There is a deep ditch on the north side of it. You will know it."

After each sentence I stopped so she could repeat the directions to Achak. Then I continued.

"Stay on this road until you have gone past

a house with a large stone chimney on the north side. Keep going for a while more until there is a road that turns north. You will see a large clump of green willow trees on the corner. Take that road. After about a half a mile you will see a green gooseberry bush on the east side of the road. Then the driveway next to it with a barbed wire gate is ours. Please ride in closing the gate behind you. Our house is made of logs. You are welcome there."

As Mary once more squeezed my hand, she turned and walked out of the store with Achak never looking back. I quietly ran to the door to watch my friend leave hoping that this would not be the last time we would meet.

After thanking Mr. Bosch for his help, I walked to the edge of town where Misty was waiting for my return. I climbed into my buggy. Once out of the field I slapped the reins on Misty's rump to tell her to head for home. She knew the way.

As she trotted along my thoughts easily went back to town to revisit my time with Mary. She too had grown older showing the signs that life had given her. I am sure she had the same thoughts of me. We were no longer the young ladies of yesterday. We had both dreamed of wearing fancy hats one day. Well, I did not own one, plain or fancy until my parcel from Ursula arrived. Mary was wearing a beautiful beaded band around her head. Her dream fulfilled, I am sure. Her moccasins were decorated with beads of different colours. She looked so small and delicate. I now needed to think of my friend as Amitola meaning Rainbow, she had said.

As I sat with my mind far away, I did not notice there was a team coming straight towards us. Misty was in the centre of the road with no intentions of moving over. As I quickly pulled on the reins she became startled wanting to pull towards the deep ditch. With much help from above I was able to keep us on the edge of the road without toppling into the ditch. When I felt the wheel drawing into the bank of the ditch, I had felt a moment of panic. I quickly reprimanded myself for daydreaming with so much at stake. Using all my might I was able to pull an excited Misty to a stop.

Looking around to apologize to the other driver, I was surprised to see that he had kept on going. I had been too shaken up to even notice if it was someone I had met before. As I settled my nerves, I looked more closely at how near I had come to having such a terrible accident. The possibility of falling into this deep ditch filled with cold water gave me the shivers. I could not begin to imagine what could have happened to Misty. This not only would have been a terrible loss to our farm family, but a replacement we could never have afforded and yet must have. It was like Misty was mine, sometimes my freedom. Now I must give her a gentle slap to let her know we must be on our way once again leaving this fright behind us. I am so grateful Misty cannot talk or for sure she would share her harrowing experience with Floyd and Buck.

Chapter Thirty-Five

It was some days later that I was in the barn-yard cleaning out the chicken house on a beautiful sunny day. Fritz and Katrin were with me washing their water dishes and refilling them with the fresh well water when I heard the sound of the Indian ponies coming. Before I could call Floyd, he came hurrying out of the barn with a smile the size of our farm on his face.

"Emma, do you hear that?" he called to me.

After waiting for this special moment for so long, I was now frozen to the ground. It was as though time had stopped, no one moved.

Just as I felt that I was wakening from a deep sleep, two chestnut ponies with shining coats and black manes came galloping towards me. It was Achak and Amitola, or were my eyes deceiving me. Maybe I am dreaming.

As Floyd stepped forward to welcome them Achak dismounted in one fluid motion as though he had wings, saying hello in his Cree language. Then Amitola slid down to stand beside her pony waiting for the sign from her husband to speak to me. With only one word, she walked towards me wearing a beautiful smile showing off her sparkly blue eyes and shiny white perfectly shaped teeth that she always had.

After a couple minutes of introductions, Achak began to relax. He slowly walked over to the corral casting the reins over the top rail. As he walked back towards Floyd he stopped to speak to Fritz and Katrin. While I do not know what he said, the gesture put them both at ease. I knew they were in awe having a real live Indian with his long braided hair standing before them.

I was amazed how quickly Floyd was able to communicate with Achak. Amitola spoke a few words to each Fritz and Katrin before turning her attention fully to me. They both stood still smiling up to her with eyes wide open as though to say are you real. We had talked about what was appropriate to say if Amitola should visit, but what would come out of a child's mouth when they are full of excitement and nervousness no one knows. I was afraid to think of it.

We slowly walked towards the garden, which seemed to capture her gaze. We both admired the flowers making a pretty fence around the vegetables. I am sure this reminded her of home as it did me. I picked two daisy blossoms placing one in her hair and the other in mine. Another reminder of our time spent together as girls. A memory of Sunday afternoons spent together in our mother's gardens now feeling a little homesick and yet grateful for this time together.

As I was about to choose some vegetables for her, she shook her head. With a smile she pointed to the red rhubarb with its large lacy green leaves and then we both laughed. I knew she too was remembering how we would pick a stalk from our gardens to munch on as we walked around sharing our secrets as we enjoyed it's tart taste making faces. After sending Katrin to the house for the butcher knife, I cut some stalks for her. She was so happy so could not stop smiling as she held them tight to her chest like they were a precious gift.

I asked her if I could meet her children one day soon. Yes, in town was her soft reply. Then again I saw tears begin to form in her eyes.

"What is the matter?" I gently asked.

"It hurts me so much to see how hard you have had to work. I see it in your face. Will it always be like this for you?"

"Yes, Mary, sorry Amitola, as long as we live here it will be a hard life. Come see our house."

I wanted to change the subject before I shared my deep secret with her just as I used to do. As we wandered through the silvery birch trees to the front of the house we both seemed to be trying to find a way to say what we were feeling. I really wanted to ask if her life was now a good one, and so I did. I could not let this opportunity pass without at least trying.

"Yes. Achak and his people are very kind to me," she said. "Achak still loves me very much. He is a good husband and father."

"Oh Amitola, I am so glad to hear that. You look well. I am happy for you, my friend."

"Only I would so like to see my mother and my father but Chief Barefoot say no. He is a kind and generous man but must be obeyed. It is their way. He says I must put that part of my life behind me, but here I am with you. Maybe one day."

"I understand. I am so grateful to have this time with you. My heart feels better. Maybe I could meet your children too. I would like that very much."

Amitola nodded as we entered our little log house. Once inside I showed her my Seidelberg Hand Crank sewing machine. It was black and old but I was so proud of it. I told her how Katrin is now learning to sew on it. She has already learned how to do embroidery work I proudly said. This brought smiles and seemed to lighten her heart.

"Ashenee will make something for her hair with her beads."

"That would be so nice. Katrin would like that," I said. "Katrin will give Ashenee a hankie that she has made. They too will be friends just like we are."

As Amitola said yes, she placed her right hand on her heart. I knew she meant forever friends. All I could do was smile. We were both so overcome with joy.

In the next instant Achak stood beside us. How could he have walked in without the old uneven floorboards creaking like they do for us, I wondered. These people truly do walk softly upon this earth. This is an art they learn at a very young age. Maybe that is why they speak softly. They also teach their young people to never sit while their elders stand. They have such good wisdom.

After taking a quick look around, he turned and walked outside with Amitola following close behind. Floyd and I too followed wondering what they were now thinking.

With not a second to waste, they both mounted

their beautiful ponies. Sitting tall on the blanket, Amitola smiled down at me still holding her bundle of rhubarb to her chest as though it were a precious gift.

In seconds my family and I were watching them ride off as though they were chasing a rainbow. We all waited until we no longer could hear the sound of their ponies echoing through the lush brush beside the road before we moved. As I turned and walked towards the house, I heard Floyd tell the children to stay away, giving me time to be alone. My tears that now flowed softly were mixed with the joy of having seen my friend and sadness of the reminder of my life ahead.

As Sundays were a day of rest doing only what was necessary, we tried to take this time to rebuild or spirits in one way or the other. The animals were milked, fed and watered. Little cooking was done. This was a day for bread and cold chicken. The afternoons sometimes were spent going to church, visiting neighbours or friends. Sometimes just being home on the farm each in our own quiet way and place.

In a couple weeks we visited the Faust family on a pleasant Sunday afternoon. While the men looked over the crops and the barnyard, the children played in the straw stack. When they tired of climbing, they threw straw at each other as they ran around the barnyard.

Bertha and I were busy making our Root beer that we had been planning for weeks and weeks. Root beer is a soft drink. Bertha had the herb mixture of root bark, leaf and spices boiled and filtered waiting to be used. After warming the mixture again we added sugar and molasses. As we stirred it waiting to be dissolved we talked of the fun we would have at the rodeo. Then we let it cool so we could add some ginger bug, transfer it into some brown bottles leaving it to ferment at room temperature. When it would reach the right amount of carbonation, Bertha will place it in a bucket lowering it into the well until it is sitting in the cold water. The cold will prevent it from fermenting any further. This was sounding more and more like a treat from heaven. We could not wait, but we must. The rodeo would not be for two more weeks.

Today is rodeo day! Weatherwise, it was not the best but our excitement was sure to make up for it. We hurriedly finished our chores, changed our clothes and set out for Weesp. We would meet our friends on the north side of the Rodeo grounds. The grassy bank was still soft with the lush green grass like that of a carpet to sit on. The horses would have plenty to eat as they waited for us. It was but a short while later that we saw the bright red wagon pulled by two high-spirited horses pulling up along side us. Our friends had arrived.

We had just laid our blankets down and were about to sit on them when we heard the incredibly loud sound of the air horn signalling the start of the events. Then there was a thunderous applause from the crowd as they welcomed the cowboys and cowgirls in their colourful western shirts riding around the ring on excited beautifully groomed horses. Two pretty ladies wearing white Stetsons riding their palominos as a bandstand full of people cheered them on carried flags.

Katrin watched with eyes large and full of awe. As Fritz took her hand, Floyd quickly reached out and grabbed his arm. We both knew they were heading for the fence. The disappointment on their faces when we explained they could not go closer nearly broke my heart. Once again they would have to watch from afar. As Floyd whispered to me how he was sure they would have been over that fence before we could reach them, I had to agree. They were too quick. They were both good at climbing.

For the most part we were close enough to see the horses as they bucked high and hard trying their best to throw their riders to the dirt covered ground. The crowd clapped and cheered as the cowmen defied them, some winning and some not. Brushing the dust off their hats and pants seemed to bring smiles to their faces as though this was what they had come for.

My favourite was the ladies barrel racing. I too was in awe of these small ladies urging their mounts on at full speed to complete a clover leaf pattern around three barrels in the fastest time without knocking over a barrel. This was truly a crowd pleaser as they were on their feet whistling and shouting as they cheered their favourite competitor on. Oh how I envied them to be in the centre of this ring in front of all these fans riding a beautiful horse. So exhilarating. Dear old Misty was no comparison.

Next came the rodeo clowns in their baggy colourful clothes with red and white painted faces were definite crowd pleasers, adults and children alike. Firstly, five clowns entered the centre of the ring playfully teasing and pushing each other as they blew their whistles. After a few minutes of clowning around for the children, three frisky yearling calves were let loose in the ring. With that the clowns began to chase them. The idea was to see who could be the first to catch a calf. As they missed, falling onto the mud the children waved and called as though they knew each calf by name telling them to run faster. Fritz, Katrin, Carmen and Grace took part from outside the corral with Marvin and Floyd at their side. This event ended with Barney, one of the smallest clowns riding on the back of the largest calf as they exited the ring waving his goodbye to the youngsters with a large red plaid handkerchief earlier used to blow his nose in a rude noisy fashion that sounded like geese honking that brought gales of laughter from the children.

About half time we sat down to eat our sandwiches of greavischmultz with our much awaited Root beer to wash them down. As we each oohed and awed at this special treat we began to open our bottles. Much to our surprise as soon as the lids were loosened letting in a little air, they exploded like rockets sending this sweet sticky liquid all over our blankets and us. Marvin and Floyd sat there in stunned silence. The kids started to cry as they watched their drinks going everywhere but in their mouths. At the sight of this, Bertha and I began to laugh. What else could we do? There were enough tears shed for us too. We had not thought of the shaking in the wagon as they drove the four miles from home. Our stoneware brown and white jugs filled with cold well water saved the day.

The next event was for the under twelve year olds to ride a sheep. Who would stay on the longest without falling off into the soft dirt? Each rider received a big round of applause with help from one of the clowns to get them back on their feet and put a smile on their face. One day they too would be in the ring riding their favourite horse or perhaps trying to stay mounted on the back of a bull while the animal attempts to buck off his rider. This eight-second competition seems like forever to the riders. It is the cheering from the crowd that spurs them on as they hang on to a long braided rope fastened to the bull. This sport has been called the most dangerous eight seconds in sports for a good reason. I am sure it is.

This fun event saved our spirits. Soon we were all laughing and cheering to the roar of the crowd forgetting about our sticky clothes. Bertha and I would each have some extra work to do tomorrow. Marvin and Floyd would both need to help us with our regular chores so we could be back onto our regular routine Tuesday.

Now it was the amazing trick riding part of the show. A handsome man wearing a black cowboy hat galloped around the ring as he stood on his mount's back holding the reins with one hand and waving to the fans with the other. The next stunt rider was a lady wearing a bright blue shirt with matching pants on a beautiful high-spirited pinto. As she sprinted around the ring with one foot in the stirrup, the other on top of the saddle, hanging upside down from the side of her horse attached by only a strap, her hair swept the dirt below drawing the crowd to their feet. Another outstanding show of horsemanship was a cowboy wearing a silver shirt with arms stretched wide as his partner in a pretty pink shirt sat on his shoulders with hands on her hips.

The last trick rider wore a suit of black standing on two white horses, one foot on each as he fearlessly galloped around the ring. When the competitors had finished their performances, a young teenage girl rode into the ring, stopped in the centre, dismounted, stepped to the front, both her and her horse took a deep bow to thank the fans for coming to see them. The roar from the crowd was so loud the announcer could not be heard giving his message.

Now it was time for the chuck wagon races. What a show they put on.

This is a team event led by a driver and either two or four outriders each. Four thoroughbred horses pull each chuck wagon, an old-fashioned canvas covered wagon. There are usually three or four teams in each race.

First an outrider must throw a barrel, representing a stove, into the back of the wagon at the sound of the starting horn. Then they mount their horse and follow the wagon to complete a figure eight around two barrels before circling a race-track.

Typically the first team to cross the finish lines wins although various penalties can be handed out ranging from a barrel knocked over to the outrider crossing the finish line too far behind his wagon driver.

The great driving skills and strength of these magnificent horses leaving a cloud of dust and dirt behind is a great finale to this fun filled event.

Now it is time to pack up our blankets and return to our farms for chores of which there never seems to be an end. As we drove home I dreamed that one day we would be able to go inside the gate, sit in the rickety grandstand of wood slats and treat ourselves to shiny red candy apples.

Chapter Thirty-Six

After returning from our trip to the rodeo, Fritz begged for a piece of rope to pretend he was the greatest lasso cowboy in our community as he ran around the corral swinging his rope. This was not anywhere near the right kind of rope. It was so thick he could barely swing it let alone make a circle but he kept on trying. It was apiece left over from when Floyd made a swing under the large pine tree near the house when we moved here. The rope had broken several times. Floyd repaired it by tying a strong knot to hold it together. Perhaps we will be able to find a rope when we visit Melvin and Imogene next time, but was careful not to mention this. I knew he would be telling Marvin all about the rodeo during our visit. It seemed Melvin had everything and more a child could possibly need.

As for Katrin, she too ran around the corral pretending she was riding the most beautiful pony. She would have pretty clothes and a white cowgirl hat. She showed us how she would wave to the fans. She constantly spoke of training her pony to do many tricks. I did not wish to spoil her dreams by telling her very few girls are able to have a pony. Their job is to do housework and cook for the family. For now she can pretend, at least for as long as I hold out hope there will be a better life for us.

A few days later it was early after supper when I saw Gary Jenkins walking along the road towards our farm as I was going to the barn to finish my chores. Now what could he want, I wondered.

After a few minutes of pleasantries I firmly suggested to Fritz and Katrin that we go to the house. They could play there. This is probably just men talk anyway. Reluctantly they ran ahead to find something to do. They already know if they whine about nothing to do they will be given some chores. That has always been a sure cure for a case of the whines.

It was long after dark before Floyd came in for the night. I could easily tell there was something bothering him. Immediately I wondered if either or both Fritz and Katrin were having a problem at school. As I knew that Fritz was likely still awake eagerly listening for a report, I kept on knitting a sweater I was remaking for Katrin.

As I watched Floyd at the washstand cleaning Misty's bridal I told him of what I was knitting. He asked as many questions as he could to keep this conversation going as he too kept a close watch on Fritz not wanting to draw his attention. Periodically Floyd would bring in a halter or something just for distraction so I asked him no questions. He would return it to the barn before the children were up in the morning.

Soon it became most apparent that the Sand Man had taken over. Fritz was sound asleep. Just for good measure we gave him another couple minutes.

"Gary told me that he overheard a couple older boys talking during recess that they had seen Bernie hanging out at Booter's place," said Floyd.

"Who is Booter?" I asked.

"He is the bootlegger that has a small shack in the woods on the northeast side of the Wallace farm."

"Oh. What do you suppose these boys are doing hanging around there?"

"I have no idea but I did suggest to Gary that perhaps he should visit their parents just to be sure they are not getting mixed into something no good. I am surprised that Booty, his dog, did not put the run on them. Something just does not seem right to me."

"I agree. That does not sound like a good place for any of our young people to be visiting. It is some time now since Bernie left home with no word. You know, the last time we were in town as I walked to our wagon I noticed a man in dark clothing with a most unkempt look standing outside the back of the barn. Could this be Booter?"

"Yes, it very likely could have been from what I have heard."

Just as I was starting to say to Floyd that the wind that had come up this evening and felt as though there was a storm brewing, I heard the first real howl as this storm began to grow. A dark curtain had begun to fall over the sky as I finished my chores so I was not too surprised. The leaves on the trees were turning over as they blew showing their fury. For sure there was about to be a heavy rain tonight. It is feeling cold enough that it just might leave some hail behind. While most of our crops were already harvested, there was still some work to be done. The good part of the cool fall weather arriving was that the mosquitoes had left for the winter. How nice it is to go to bed at night without them buzzing around our faces trying to land in our ears for their evening feast.

By the time we were ready to turn in for the night, the door was shaking from the blowing wind. We would need to prop a chair holding a couple blocks of firewood for added weight against it to prevent it from opening as we sleep. A hungry coyote would be just too happy to come inside looking for a meal.

As I climbed under the covers I told myself to not sleep too soundly so as to hear any signs of danger during the night. It was only a matter of minutes when the Sand Man had taken control of me too with his mighty spell. All that was left for me were my dreams of a beautiful angel dressed in sparkling white carrying a plate of my favourite ginger nut cookies just baked by my mother. I could even smell them.

I awoke to the sound of the door creaking. As I leapt out of bed I realized that Floyd was already up, it must have been him going to the barn to do chores. I could hear the rain pounding outside the window as the wind continued to blow angrily. First I must slow my heart down to it's regular beat. By the time I was dressed I felt that I was once again back to normal. Time to put coffee and water on to heat.

In a short while I was off to the barn to begin my morning chores. Much to my dismay the ground was now a saturated mess of sand and just plain heavy muddy dirt. The brown rye grass was lying on its' side as if it had taken a hard beating from both rain and wind. I wondered what the remainder of our crops were looking like today. Poor Floyd. His hours and hours of hard work may be gone with nothing left to be saved. I will need to bring the last of the vegetables in the garden inside where they will stay in the cellar. Thankfully there is very little left to bring in. The last of the turnips and cabbage I had brought in a few days earlier. While I was so very tired that night, I am now feeling grateful that I was able to finish as much as I did.

Like many of my neighbours, the farmer women raised as many of their chicks themselves as they were able. Chicks take twenty-one days to hatch. The brooder hen will take care of any eggs that will not hatch into viable chicks. One rooster for about twenty chickens is all that is needed. No wonder roosters are happy to wake in the morning bright and early. There are more chickens in the world than any other species of birds. Should a farmer require more baby chicks, they are available for purchase at the local feed stores. Due to the cost, we purchased very few. I had made a small nursery to keep the baby chicks warm and safe until they were old enough to be with the remainder of our flock.

As I grew up as a teenager I was able to gain some knowledge on raising these soft downy fluffy little balls growing into gawky pullets. Small white leghorn pullets are the best for laying eggs. It was both necessary and difficult to maintain a warm even temperature in the coop. Chickens do not have teeth so it is necessary to keep a watchful eye on their food supply. Letting them run loose to peck for themselves not only makes for a happy chicken, but a healthy one with rich egg yolks firmly raised. It is not long before the baby chicks will run to their mother when she calls them. It is a natural chicken thing. I will not need to think of baby chicks again until spring.

There were still a couple chickens that I had raised for meat to butcher and can for dinners. This too must be done within the next few days. Our laying hens were healthy. They had been providing enough eggs each day for our use. Occasionally there would be enough to sell a few to one of our town folk. Along with the few sales of cream, this brought me a little spending money for next year's chicks as well as to tuck away a few coins for my future dream.

This past spring had been a fortunate one for us. Our clover fields were tall and healthy beside our rolling fields of barley and oats. The bee man said this year's crop of honey was the sweetest and most plentiful he had reaped for several years. This meant a little more income for us. He would be back again next year with as many or more hives.

It was now time to remove the sticky fly strips hanging inside our little home dropping them into the hot fire to hear them snap and crackle as they disappear going up into the smoke filled chimney. Next spring we will need to hang some new ribbons made with a scented glue formula designed to catch even the largest of horse flies.

Chapter Thirty-Seven

Christmas is approaching with little difference in our lives from previous years. Klaus did not arrive last fall as I had hoped. While I thought of it daily, I tried to not show my disappointment.

Each day as I milked the cows, I freely let my mind wander to the day we were in town when Amitola and Achak walked toward me with their three children. I relived each and every moment of that day as I pictured their faces and listened to each voice softly speaking in a firm manner with few words. I want to never forget one second of this special time.

Ashenee, meaning angel, the oldest looking so much like her pretty mother I could not miss her. She truly looked like a little angel ready for flight. Kitchi, meaning brave, did not look to be any younger although I knew from his grandma that there was a year difference. Just like Fritz and Katrin. Then I was introduced to Kanti, meaning sings, the youngest child. Right on queue, Fritz and Katrin appeared at this perfect moment followed by Floyd.

Within seconds Katrin asked for her hankies with the little pink flowers she had carefully embroidered to give to the girls. Ashenee and Kanti clearly showed their love for their gifts with big smiles for Katrin. With a nod of approval from me, Amitola removed

Katrins' hat and nodded to Ashenee. With the sweetest smile she placed, a little crookedly, a colourful beaded headband on Katrin's head. Amitola was quick to adjust it for Katrin. The huge smile on her face said it all. She loved it. We both explained to our daughters that they are now friends just like their mothers. They shyly held hands for a moment. I knew this was a special moment that neither would forget.

Floyd and Fritz had their great moment too. Achak motioned for them to follow him and Kitchi outside. Amitola said that he wanted to show his ponies to Floyd. I could tell that Fritz was so excited he was nearly bursting at the seams as they walked together to South Road.

Whenever a few shoppers walked by, their attention immediately turned to us with a strange look on their faces. This was not a common sight in Weesp. The Cree people and the white man were not known to associate in a friendly manner. I knew we would be the talk of the town. All I cared about was my friend. They did not know that this lady was my friend. They did not know that she grew up on a farm with a loving mother and father. They did not know of her heritage. They did not know of her caring and loving heart. They did not know that love could find you in the strangest places.

We quickly shared our feelings of spending these brief moments together. They were so special to both of us. We spoke of being homesick, not just for each other but for our families as well. She told me how Abe is still her close companion but getting older with each harsh winter. I wanted to know but did not wish to ask if her children have learned to ride. With Katrin standing there wanting a horse so much, I was afraid of the tears that just might follow showing her broken heart. Without my asking, I was told they would be moving on for the winter. I had known this was their way even though I was wishing that just this one year it would not happen.

Much too soon our husbands and sons returned. It was time for them to leave. As I stood on the uneven dilapidated sidewalk watching my friend walk away, I somehow felt this would be the last time we would meet. Oh, please let me be wrong. For now I shall savour every moment of our time together. It shall be tucked away in a special corner of my heart forever.

Now it was time for us to make the walk to the livery stable field where Buck and Misty were waiting. I knew it was too cold for Katrin to be outside without a hat but she was so happy with her new beaded headband I just had to let her be until we were at least out of town. I felt like that when I wore my hat from Ursula for the first time. One day my daughter will make a fine lady wearing a fancy hat with gloves to match. For now she will continue to ask me when she can have mitts with fingers.

It was again that time of year when I would go to the Little School House twice a week to help the teacher and students prepare for their Christmas Concert. The last evening of school before the Christmas break parents and neighbours would gather in the Little School House for this special evening. First there is much work to be done.

Each year there is a special performance by each of the community schools in the Cold Cut District. This year it was decided that we should participate. While the students are practicing for our concert, they could practice one more song for this special Winter Festival. Mr. Swain volunteered to pick up the students, teacher and myself in his sleigh. Not having a variety of music to choose from, it was decided that we would sing The Church in the Wildwood. This is a song written in 1857 following a coach ride. The church was said to be in a valley near a small country town. In later years the church became known as the Little Brown Church.

Being a popular song among the adults it was thought to be pleasing to the judges. Practice began each and every day. Having several students with strong voices I was sure we could pull this off. I am not sure if the students were more excited to have a day out or to have a hour long sleigh ride to the Prairie Range District. Mr. Swain said he had bells to put on the harnesses of his team for added fun.

After weeks of diligent practice December came. It was time to perform. With one last practice and a strong reminder to be at school no later than eight in the morning, lunch pails in hand excitement had filled our one room school to overflowing.

In the morning I rose at five thirty eager to get my chores done. Floyd was just crawling out of his warm bed as I walked to the stove to get the fire crackling. I looked out the window expecting to see the morning sky rising to a bright gold where the sun would be waiting to shine upon us. Alas, my worst fears had arrived. We were having a blizzard.

The outside world looked like one huge snowdrift. With the winds blowing dropping the temperature even more with such force the drifts were already deep and getting deeper as I watched with a sinking heart. There would be no concert for us.

At regular time I woke Katrin and Fritz. As they both sat up instantly eager to get their day underway, I gave them the disappointing news. With tears in their eyes, they both lay back down pulling the blanket over their faces to hide their sadness. How could Mother Nature be so cruel I wondered? These students had so little to look forward to in their lives, now this too was taken from them.

Each year all the students would join together to sing two songs. The first one would be part way through the program, the other to close the evening followed by "We Wish You a Merry Christmas". Only one year was we so fortunate to have a teacher that was able to play the not too well tuned piano. I took on the task of teaching them both the words and the tune by following me. I am in no way a great singer, but I can carry a tune quite well so along with a few students that were quick learners we managed very nicely. The School Board only provided one sheet of paper with words and music on it. I could not read music. As I looked at it I felt

I could tell when the tune became higher or lower. With Bossy for comfort I went over and over it as I did my milking. I must make this a tune and so I kept at it.

First I needed to learn the words. Then in the same way the students needed to learn the words by repeating after me. While I am trying to do this, the teacher is busy trying to keep the unruly boys in hand.

When the teacher felt the students needed a break, we would work with them to put together a play. This kept the active ones a little more under control. The students that did not have a part in the play were given recitations. Everyone must be involved. They too needed help to learn their lines.

Each year the teacher would write a copy to be given to each student with their part. As many as could be trusted were to take it home, and back, for their parents to help them. With many parents not being able to read, this was a task that at the beginning seemed impossible. Somehow each year it came together beautifully. Each year I prayed that God would help us prepare. Each year He did.

With Floyd having an ear for music, he was able to help me get the tune by playing on his fiddle. As there were other students besides Katrin that could not carry a tune but must be involved, they needed to be gently asked to sing softly.

Each year when we began to prepare, I felt that it would be an eternity before this program was any where near being heard. Before I knew it, the time was here. As in the years before, each student came through like the shinning stars they were. To be able to watch their overly proud parents was an excitement of its own. They clapped, smiled and laughed with the students as they stood some so tall and proud with others so shy.

Abner was a boy with a constant big smile that was very excitable. As he walked one way, he looked the other. As of yet, he has not grown into his bigger than average feet. This could be counted on to have an added effect each year be it in the play or with just his presence. Each year we looked forward to what he would add that would be sure to bring a chuckle or two. I felt he made the program special.

When the students gathered together at the front and finished their last song, they each gave a big bow to their audience. The clapping and cheering went on for an extra long time this year bringing the biggest smiles to their proud faces. This was a great reward for their hard work. They had surely earned it. Then the parents began calling The Church in the Wildwood over and over. With the greatest eagerness I led them in the song they had learned so well. They each stood proud and tall as they sang their hearts out. They had just performed for those that appreciated it most. The standing ovation they received will stay in their memories for years to come.

Before leaving to go home with their families, each student was given a bag of treats consisting of an orange, a few hard ribbon candies and some peanuts in the shell by someone from the School

District.

When the desks were replaced and ready for classes to begin after the holidays, goodbyes were said with many thanks to the teacher for patience and hard work. As we drove home in the dark, shining eyes could be seen watching us as we travelled past the packs of coyotes checking us out. As we drove I held up the lantern that Floyd had lit before we left the schoolyard. This kept them from approaching our wagon.

When we reached our log house, Floyd would stop in front and wait while I went inside and lit the lamp. Then he was able to take the lantern with him to the barn as he settled the team in for the night. Many a night when he came inside he said he could hear them milling about in the bush near the barn watching him, sometimes letting him see their glowing eyes.

Just as in past years, this is the time of the year that I get reminded of just how snowed in and alone we are. Now is the time that I should be baking and making other preparations for Christmas. Again this year there will not be anything special. No baking, no presents, no treats. I will as in past years insist on a Christmas tree. They are free to us on our farm. Our house will have the smell of pine.

Finally it was but a few days before Christmas. The sun was shining, the snow was deep and crisp. After lunch I announced that Fritz, Katrin and I would be going to the bush for our Christmas tree. The temperature was around thirty-five below at this time of the year.

Each year I would try to pick a day when the wind was low and the bright sun high in the sky giving us its' warmth. Today would be as perfect as it will get.

As we dressed in our boots and parkas, Floyd reminded us each to be extra careful. He would tell Fritz and Katrin to stay out of momma's way when she is chopping. Of course they always promised they would. He would be in the barn should we need to find him. As soon as Katrin finished hugging her dad we would be on our way.

With axe in hand, I set out with Fritz and Katrin following close behind. I needed to make a path for them where they could follow in my footsteps. At this time of the year, the snow was nearing their waists. As we trudged the half-mile to the bush they kept up a steady chatter of how beautiful the tree was going to be this year. It would always be better than last year. With their anticipation of finding the perfect tree, they did not notice the difficult walk. I could tell by the tone of their voices if they were getting tired. When I felt that I needed to give them a moment to rest I stopped to let them know that I was the one that needed a short rest. They would assure me I would be fine as they patiently waited.

As we wandered around inside the bush area checking each tree for its perfect branches, I had to remind them not to go too far into the dense forest. We also checked to be sure there was no sign of bird nests in the trees that they may wish to return to. We would then talk of how these nests are their homes for their babies next year. While they both watched for bunny tracks so as to not disturb their homes either, I kept my eye out for larger tracks of bigger wild animals. I did not wish to encounter a wolf or a coyote or even a fox. A fox can look friendly but when getting too close they can be very nasty, and not just their smell. We would need to carry our tree out and then home. Eventually a decision was made. We found it, we found it, they would shout. I knew that would be the one. If we had nothing else, we would have the perfect tree.

With all my might I would swing the axe into the sturdy trunk of the rich pine tree. As I moved around chopping at each side, I was grateful that I had built up mussels from farming. Like other women in our community, I wished I had dainty arms every time I put a dress on. This was not the time. As I caught my breath before leaving, I enjoyed the fresh scent of the pine forest. Then it was time to head for home. Chores were waiting. Soon the bright sky will begin to grow dimmer as it prepares for night. Nature's wildlife will then have their time in the fields undisturbed by humans.

First of all, we took turns emptying the snow from our boots and mitts. As I picked up the axe in my left hand with my right hand holding the tree trunk, I would hear Fritz saying I've got it. Then Katrin would say the same holding the top of the tree. We were ready.

Much too soon I noticed the sky turn from its golden light to a pale pink telling me that we must try to hurry. There was surely going to be a fresh blanket of snow before darkness set in for the night.

With several stops to rest our arms, we hurried along. Fluffy white flakes were starting to fall threatening to cover our path as we neared the farm. It would not be long before there would be a sheet of white before our eyes. We kept our steady pace up as we raced mother nature home.

The task of placing our tree against the house under the birch trees was as big as carrying it out of the forest. The untouched snow had piled itself up as high as my waist with a crusty top from the freezing nights. This was a task for a shovel.

Later that evening after chores were completed, we sat near the stove to keep warm. There was still a chill in our bones. This was the time for Fritz and Katrin to tell Floyd all about the forest. They loved to talk of how tall the trees were. They would exclaim how there were so many trees no one could count that high. When they finished relaying the afternoon event over and over again, they asked me to tell the story of Grey Wolf that I had told them so often when they were little. It had become our Winter Story. Sometimes I would try to leave a little out just to shorten it but they knew it so well that no matter how tired they were, they wanted the full story. Floyd always agreed with them, so with three against one I would begin again where I had decided to shorten it. Floyd thought I should never let them forget this time in our lives. So from then on until spring this would much too often be our evening story.

Chapter Thirty-Eight

At long last we had a Pastor that came to the schoolhouse in the next community once a month. This meant a five-mile trip, not the summer only thirty-mile trip that took us from morning until evening. This was one that Buck and Misty could do with their steady walk. Our Christmas service was held on Christmas Eve day at one in the afternoon. Again there was a concert involving all the children. This time all the preparations were done at home. The mothers took turns looking after the program.

When this special day arrived, recitations were said, songs were sung. There was no piano. One member of the congregation sang with them to help keep the tune. Again I reminded Katrin to sing softly so her voice would sound much prettier. Two or three children would sing together a Christmas Carol without so much as a moments practice together. They each performed like it was something they did everyday as children always do. Then each child was given a brown bag with an orange, some ribbon candies and peanuts. Treats like these were always taken home to be shared with their families.

After wishing our church friends a Merry Christmas we would head for home. One year we went to spend the remainder of the day and evening at the Faust home. They next year they came to our home.

While the men took care of the necessary

chores, Bertha and I prepared dinner. Canned chicken, boiled potatoes, canned carrots and peas with homemade bread was our Christmas dinner. The most special part was having it with our friends. We all enjoyed being together more than anything else. No ginger nut cookies.

While Bertha and I cleaned up the dishes, the children sat on the floor playing their games of String. The men were at the barn checking on the horses.

Soon either Floyd or Marvin, depending on whose turn it was, would come inside explaining the other would be along shortly. He would always be checking on one of his cows. The children never caught on.

In a couple minutes the sound of sleigh bells could be heard in the distance. As we all listened they came louder and louder until they were outside the house where we could hear the familiar Ho Ho Ho again and again. The children stared at the door with their eyes wide open as they stood in awe. When Santa was invited inside with his large sack over his shoulder the children jumped up and down shouting Hi Santa! Hi Santa!

At this time Santa and us three adults made a big fuss over how either Floyd or Marvin was missing Santa. One of us even looked out the door to see if we could see him coming.

After Santa's questions as to who was good and who had been bad he then directed the same questions to us adults to which he had funny comments to go with our prepared answers. Then it was time for Santa to find something special in his sack for the children (a popcorn ball) with a promise to return next year. Hugs were given followed by shouts of By Santa, see you next year and he was off to find his reindeer waiting for him in the field.

As the children unwrapped their treat, Bertha and I quickly took the paper from them before they could put it in the cook stove to burn. We needed to save it for next year. Hiding this special paper was another reason to have large pockets on our aprons.

Soon either Floyd or Marvin would come inside complaining about one of the cows being stubborn to find that he had just missed Santa. As the children all clambered over him to show him their treat, he would pretend to take a nibble from each popcorn ball to see if he knew which one was the tastiest. Finally it was decided that they were all the best. Maybe next year I will be able to tell which one it is, he would say.

Soon the time came in the evening when it was time to go home. The horses were hitched to the sleigh as we all shouted Merry Christmas to each other. For the rest of the evening I felt the comfortable warm glow of having such dear friends. They made Christmas complete. Knowing this was Jesus' time; we would celebrate His birthday tomorrow with prayer. We would give our thanks for His grace and mercy. For His continual and unconditional forgiveness. Tonight was about sharing this special time with friends.

Chapter Thirty-Nine

Epiphany, the celebration to remember the three wise men's visit to baby Jesus and his baptism has now come and gone. Today is the day when school should be starting again. It has been snowing each and every day since Christmas. This morning when I awoke, I could hear the wind blowing. Once again Jack Frost had left his beautiful designs on the inside of each of our windows. Looking out all I could see was white. Thinking it was the frosted windows; I slowly scraped a patch large enough to see outside as I began to wake up. Much to my dismay, the white was snow. We were having a blizzard. The wind was blowing strong and furious as the snow swirled and blew first one way and then it swirled as it flew the other piling the snow into large banks.

With my heart so heavy that it was resting on my knees, I made my way to the stove. I would need to keep the fire burning strong and steady to keep us warm. There would be no venturing any further from the house and barn than necessary. There would be no school today. Today was the day I had planned to bake a pot of beans. I had put them on to soak last night. I saw where Floyd had taken the washbasin and set it near the very back of the stove. For some reason a little water had been left in it. It had frozen as we slept.

I could see nothing in this day to change my feelings for this godforsaken country. During the holidays I had promised myself to be grateful for what we had, even if it was barely enough to survive. It will get better. Now I knew that it was just a vicious circle. This year will be like the last, and the one before, and the one before.

After spending the last three days enduring a blizzard, I woke to a calm sky. The wind had settled down to a gentle breeze. Today we must dig ourselves out.

As soon as breakfast was over, Floyd harnessed Buck to help him break a path to the house from the barn. Then a wider path to the wood pile, a proper path to the outhouse and then to the road. The children would not go to school today but for sure they must go tomorrow.

Buck and Misty were both draft horses but Buck being a little bigger liked to feel that he led the way. They both were now wearing their winter coats of long black thick hair with fluffy white socks. They loved the cold crisp air.

It was time to stop for lunch by the time the children and I had the path finished to the wood pile. The path to the outhouse was wide enough for one. More was not needed. I used our galvanized shovel while the children each used a smaller shovel that Floyd had built for them from slabs given to him from Melvin. The wood box and the coal bin were so empty I could see bottom. Today we must split wood and replenish our inside supply. First we must clear the snow from the woodpile. While I split, the children will carry it inside. The kindling and wood will need to be thawed before it can be burned.

Before we began to split and carry wood, we went into the house to warm our feet and hands. Boots and mitts were put on the oven door to warm. Wet socks were replaced with dry ones leaving the wet to dry for the evening chores. A piece of bread with a cup of hot water satisfied our tummies.

Morning came with another nice day in store. When it was time for the children to leave for school, I walked to the road with them. There Fritz said I should go to the house, they would be fine. I worried that they may walk too close to the edge of the road and fall into the ditch. It could still be soft under the top crust. So I kissed them goodbye and headed to the house stopping half way there to watch them through the trees.

As I stood in my hiding place, I could see two small people in their black winter parkas trudging along until they were so small I could not see them anymore. I knew they would be there in a short while. Mr. Jenkins would be able to see them now as he stood at his window watching for his students to arrive. By now I could see others walking the same road for their day's lessons. Their education did not come easy.

As I went about finishing my morning outdoor chores, I noticed that Floyd was so content as he went about his chores. I felt he was truly at peace with his life. I was not.

By mid-morning I felt I needed to go inside. My feet and hands were so cold I was beginning to fear for frostbite. When I got inside, I began to empty the snow from my boots, then I would sit with my feet on the warm oven door for a few minutes. My father always told us to pull ourselves up by our bootstraps whenever we were feeling down. Well dad, these boots are nearly worn out with no straps to pull. Each fall I make new liners for the bottoms of our boots from scraps of yarn and old coats that are too small for Katrin.

Until it is time to make lunch for Floyd and I, I shall continue to try to think of ways that I could earn a little money to add to my small stash for a better life. We are physically old beyond our years. Both my parents were worn out by the time they were fifty. Like many people, that was the time for them to go to their heavenly home where they could find rest. As I worked on my knitting, I wondered how I could find the strength and courage to leave the man I still loved but would not leave with me. As my tears began to flow I wondered how my children would survive. I am the only one to help. Maybe this summer Klaus will come.

Chapter Forty

The road had now become passable. It was hard packed snow. We were able to venture out. Each night I would mark off the day on our wall calendar given to each farmer from the feed store. This told me that we were at the beginning of February. We should now be seeing some bare ground, not just snow. With the cold crisp air the sound of the owls hooting to each other can be heard throughout our farm.

The black bears, which are not closely related to either the brown or polar bears, should be leaving their den after a long winter's nap with their soft furry cubs toddling along behind. They had spent the daylight hours of the fall hunting to build up the large fat reserve they will need for hibernation. They build their dens under a hollow tree or in a burrow within a heavily wooded area. We provide plenty of that. The momma bears will now be thin and hungry and eager to protect and feed her growing cubs. She will fear no one or anything to protect her babies.

Today we had been to town. As we rode along each mile all there was to see were snow-covered trees with fields and fields of white frozen snowdrifts. It seemed as though all the farmers and their families had felt safe to venture out. There were many sleigh tracks in the frozen road telling us we were not alone.

While my heart was not in Weesp, I happily greeted my northern friends as we shared news of these past weeks. I knew the men would be discussing the spring thaw, which should soon be leaving the fields deep with cold water. They needed to think of planting their crops in order to have a rich golden field of oats and rye to harvest in the fall. This was our main livelihood.

Today, more than ever, the chugging of the train as it rolled into town seemed louder and closer than ever before. It whistled shrill and clear as though to get my attention. The steam engine train seemed to send its grey puffs high into the sky for me to see. Its' dirty coal smell permeated the air throughout town. Weesp was the end of the line.

There was no station house, just the thick forest of trees to surround the horseshoe shaped tracks to turn around and head back out of town. There it would stop for a short while should anyone wish to board taking with them their dreams of a brighter world to see. No one ever seemed to arrive, only leave. Today this giant steam locomotive sent my mind whirling with ideas. In the end, I still required money even if it is just to dream of gazing out the window as the country side flew by as I sat on a soft comfortable seat with my children making my way into a new life. Could this possibly be my way out?

Before leaving town I went to the small post office with the Union Jack flying outside high and proud, to see if there were any messages for me. Nothing. Not even a short telegram. I knew the possibilities were slim, but I was still disappointed.

When we arrived in Weesp earlier in the day,

Floyd mentioned that he planned to visit with Jimmie Hammer. Mr. Hammer was a burly man of over six foot tall with a short beard, thick unkempt dark hair that he cut himself with his 'sharp as the devil' all purpose knife. He wore a pair of well-worn overalls over his thick shirt with rolled up sleeves and large heavy work boots. A can of Copenhagen chewing tobacco filled his shirt pocket with a pinch firmly placed under his bottom lip resting against his gum. His handmade spittoon sat nearby on the top of a post next to the shed. Floyd had mentioned that going by the smell, he did not think it had ever been washed, and certainly not with lye soap.

Mr. Hammer held two coveted jobs in the south side of town. Tuesday and Thursday mornings he was the best blacksmith for miles around with a booming business. In his shed he stored his tools as well as coal bins, coal shovels, pokers and other items for sale. His shed was never locked. If a farmer came in need of a item they would take it leaving the money in the nearby bucket. If his apron was hanging on the doorway into the shed that was his sign that he had left for the day. He liked to do the forging of iron and steel before the day became too hot.

Due to the extreme heat from his fire pit, this was also the least time of the week for the young boys to hang out. When they did come to watch, they were given a few pointers on the job. A few minutes after they became restless he would look down on them from under his bushy eyebrows giving them a stern look following his warning as always, "lookee out young fellas, this ere fire is hotter'n a pistol." This quickly sent them turning on their heels for the main street of town leaving only dust behind as Jimmie wiped his forehead with a dirty rag. With a sinister chuckle that could be heard as if a warning was sent their way, his thoughts went to the next time they would be back, and they would be back.

The remainder of his six-day workweek he could be found nearby in his other blacksmith/farrier shop working hard with horses. There he spent many hours trimming their hoofs with a rasp. Sometimes he would need to adjust the metal shoes before placing the shoes on their hooves. Jimmie not only placed the shoes on but trimmed and balanced their hooves. He loved his job as farrier as much as he did eating. That was a lot. Every day it was bread, bologna and beans. I highly suspect it was hot oatmeal porridge in the mornings. He needed to eat something that stuck to his large frame, and it did stick.

As a farrier, he was a specialist in hoof care. Jimmie liked to tell how he had only gone to grade two. "All my learnen was done from dirty old Mac. He was tough and smelt it and knew it all. He show'd me how." Jimmie would say with a big grin spreading across his whiskered cheeks.

Even the most skittish of horses he could calm down. When the job was done, he fed his faithful customers a piece of carrot, scratched their forehead and moved on to the next. There was always work to do. Well, just enough to keep him busy and out of the pool hall.

On our way home Floyd was quiet. I could tell he was in deep thought. Gary Jenkins had gone to town with us but he too was quiet. Was there trouble brewing? I had not heard even a hint of unrest from any of the ladies. It was just the usual conversation within the community. Mr. Bosch had not conveyed to me a feeling of concern, just his usual warm friendly smile.

Later that evening when all was quiet in the house, Floyd said, "we need to talk." My heart fell. This must be serious.

"So what is the trouble?" I asked not wishing to wait any longer.

"There is talk around town that several farmers are missing some chickens. A cow has disappeared too. We both know that right away they think the Indians did it. They have also been talking of the Indians visiting our place. I tried to assure them of the reason. I explained of your friend when you were both just girls, how she had come to live with the Indian people. They did not steal her. I tried to say to them that Achak and Amitola were good people. I begged them to talk to Mr. Bosch before taking matters up with Officer Judd. I am not sure they will listen."

"If they do, I am sure not only Achak but also Chief Barefoot will no longer trust the white man. This may make trouble for Mr. Bosch and Amitola. Oh Floyd, do you think it was any of their doing?"

"No I don't. I do not think it is someone from

our community. I think it is more likely to be from another community where they would not be known here. And they would know the Indians are staying near Weesp so they would be the ones to get the blame."

"Do you think there is anything we can do?" I asked.

"Yes, tomorrow is Sunday. If the weather is good we will visit Marvin and Bertha. I will ask Marvin to ask around. For now we shall pray that this will not be so."

"Oh dear, I feel another sleepless night is coming for us."

When we arrived at the Faust farm, Marvin was outside by the barn so after dropping the children and I off near the house; he headed straight over to unhitch the team. Bertha came running outside to great me with her usual robust hug. Katrin always said Mrs. Faust was soft and cuddly. That was a good way to put it.

As soon as I was inside with Bertha putting the coffee on she asked if all was well. After hearing my story of Amitola she sat down heavily onto her usual chair. I could see by the serious look on her face that she too was concerned but also in disbelief.

Soon the men were inside as well ready and eager to enjoy some hot coffee. They both claimed they could smell it as its strong flavour wafted across to the corral. Where there was coffee, there was Marvin.

They had been to town, the day before us,

which for some reason was busier even than on Saturday. They too had heard of the theft problem in both our community and theirs. As far as they knew there was only one farmer that was missing some chickens.

Both Floyd and Marvin said they were sure it was not the Indians. In the past, the Indians had not left a trace of their visit. They did no harm. Not a sound had ever been heard, not even a growl from the family dog. This time there was some damage done to two of the chicken coops as well as the fence where the cow had gone missing. Marvin assured us that was not the way of the Indians but rather some restless young men that had managed some liquor from the local bootlegger and were beyond using their senses.

To blame the Indians did not make any sense to any of us. First of all they did not usually return to this reservation before the snow left. At the first sign of winter not having left, they would not have continued North.

Chapter Forty-One

Eventually the snow left, the ground was drying up, and the birch trees were showing off their silver bark. The birch trees in our area are actually a white birch but have a silvery look especially when the sun shines on them. Silver sounded prettier to us than white. It is a medium sized deciduous tree with dark leaves with a lacy edge changing into a light yellow in the fall. Their bark is dark brown at first turning into white thin papery strips making an excellent fire starter.

It is now April. The snow is all melted save for the sheltered areas in the forest protected from the mid day sun. The male bears are out roaming around the fields as they forge for food. As the plants begin to green the mother bears begin to gain energy and body fat from the willows. They have babies to feed. Cows can be seen grazing in the fields as they chew their cuds. The saying is that April showers bring Mayflowers. I sure do hope that is true, but not white ones. I have seen enough white for a while.

This year will hold the most changes in our lives since we left Estuary for the north. Our last trip to town was the most newsworthy since we arrived. Some changes were good, some not so good. Like the rest of the community, we will adjust.

Doc. Brown must retire. This much-loved man in the community has been having heart difficulties for the past few years. Doc. Murphy in Cross Cut has been advising him that he must retire for the benefit of his own health. After a lengthy search, he has located a doctor willing to move to Weesp to set up practice in mid summer.

Doc. Hugg is a middle-aged man with a perky wife with a big friendly smile and two strapping sons in high school. Neither one has an interest in medicine but rather farming. Doc. Hugg feels they both could gain much practical experience in a farming community that would not be available in the city. They are both willing and able to help a needy farmer in exchange for the experience and a drink of real cow's milk. They both would like to sleep in the hayloft if that would help, if not for the experience. They are eager to taste it all.

Mrs. Hugg is an outgoing small lady choosing to wear a long skirt and sturdy shoes with a kind and gentle heart wrapped in a comfy hand-made shawl. She has experience as a practical nurse in a hospital. Eula has delivered many babies and is eager to be of assistance in home deliveries. She has her own horse and buggy to make independent visits. This clearly looks like a great helping hand for the whole community. Perhaps not so many babies will be taken in the first few days with Eula being willing and able to stay and help care for our newborns a while longer.

Mr. Bosch feels that they will be a fit for us all. I do too. This truly is a blessing from God when they felt the need and desire to accept this request. Mrs. Hugg said she thinks they will receive more than they will be giving. I think it will be a win for Weesp and its' people as well.

The town people are saying that there is word that World War 11 will be ending real soon. There already has been too many lives lost, families torn apart and children suffering the loss of fathers and older brothers. Food is still in short supply with rationing attempts to give the poor an equal opportunity. Even with coupons, many of us do not have the means to purchase all that we need.

Now that spring is just around the corner, our sleighing accident on the way home from town is just a bad memory of reality in the North. Hopefully this will not happen again. I shall never forget that day, as I am sure others cannot forget theirs. There are too many unavoidable accidents.

It was middle of the afternoon on a cold clear Saturday that we set out with Buck and Misty for home. Floyd and I were both feeling extra happy within ourselves. It had been a time of visiting with those we enjoy spending our town time with. Everyone was in good health with no major problems. Fritz and Katrin had a fun time running through town, greeting the train engineer as he turned this giant train to once again leave for stops unknown. They both enjoyed looking in the store windows with dreams of what may someday be theirs to purchase.

As we were travelling at a steady pace past the muskeg, a coyote came leaping out of the bush barking at our horses ready to take them on. In an instant they both bolted in terror. As Floyd tried desperately to retain control over these two large draft horses, he shouted to me to throw the kinner out and then jump.

I felt a fright inside me that I had never felt before. In the next few seconds I imagined all the things that could go wrong. Would I be strong enough to throw them far enough away from the sleigh so as to not get run over? Would they get hurt as they landed on the hard packed frozen road that had yet to melt? Would Floyd be killed in this terrible accident that is about to take place? How could I jump out leaving my husband behind?

As he yelled, "Emma, do it now" I found myself moving, as if in slow motion, toward them.

I gave Fritz, as he was the oldest, a quick instruction as I took him by the arm and threw him over the side landing face down. Without so much as a whimper, Katrin was beside me with huge frightened eyes but ready to leave this speeding sleigh. I saw her fly through the air and then land on her back. With Floyd yelling, "jump Emma" I stepped over the side and jumped for all I was worth.

The ground was hard. I too landed on my back. It was as though my mind was whirling. This was surreal. Then I heard Fritz calling Katrin over and over. Where are they I asked myself? I could not see. Then he stopped calling. All was quiet.

Later Fritz told me how he picked himself up and started off to get to Katrin both running and stumbling as he tried to steady himself on the slippery road. As he reached his sister still lying on the road with eyes closed, another sleigh pulled up beside them. I did not know there was anyone else on the road. The lady wearing a big coat and fuzzy mitts jumped down to help. As she helped pick Katrin up her eyes opened. Fritz was so proud that when she saw him she smiled as she tried to get up onto her unsteady feet. They were both helped into the sleigh as this kind lady comforted them with reassurance all would be well over and over again.

Soon the sleigh and these kind people were beside me. As I came to, it took me a few minutes to put together all that had happened. With some help from the driver who spoke in Russian, I tried my best to get up on my own feet so I too could climb into their sleigh. With much ado, and help I somehow climbed over the side landing on the floor beside my kinner. That must have been quite the sight. I know I blushed as I thought of my bloomers that may have been showing. That was too personal for me.

Once again the sleigh was moving with these two caring people speaking in a language I could not understand with the exception of the odd word. When I heard whoa, whoa, I started to have more of a sense of what was happening. We had now stopped on the edge of the road. I could see our sleigh resting against some large pine trees. No sign of Floyd. Once again I am climbing over the side to get out. This time there was no worry of my bloomers showing. I did not even think of them, only Floyd.

We found Floyd with our team still hitched together. Buck was still hitched to the sleigh but Misty had broken loose. Quiet gentle Misty was in an extremely agitated state. It took both men a while to calm them down. Misty was still prancing and eager to get loose but now manageable. As for Buck, he had now stopped kicking and rearing in defiance. His legs were trembling as were Misty's as they both continued to shake their heads with an angry snort.

The two men spent the next while calming them down. Floyd said he could not have had the strength to hold them by himself much longer. He had felt he was already loosing the little control he had.

With the help of these strangers, we managed to get our team hitched to the sleigh in a makeshift fashion. I found myself praying that it would hold together for the remainder of our trip home. We still had six miles to travel and dusk was beginning to settle. For some reason we did not have the lantern with us.

Leaving Fritz to hold the reins of their team as he talked to them so as to not give them the feeling they were alone, we three adults helped pull on the sleigh as Floyd coaxed the team backwards. There was no room to turn around. They had to leave the way they came. This would have been a feat in itself but with two upset strong horses it was more difficult.

Floyd hung onto their halters as he walked them backwards talking softly to them with hopes of giving them reassurance that they were safe. Had they bolted again he would surely have been trampled.

After praises to Fritz for doing a young mans' job so well while he was still a boy, we shook hands thanking them over and over for their kindness. We were not sure if they were able to understand our heartfelt words but feel they did. We were able to feel their kindness too. This we will never forget.

While we were nervous heading out onto the roads where there would likely be no other travellers, we were happy to be on our way. We still had to hurry before the darkness completely descended upon us.

By the time we reached our farm, it was just on the verge of being too dark to safely travel without a light. Stopping outside the door of our home, I quickly went inside to get the lantern for Floyd. Yes, it was on the floor just inside the door right where he had left it. That is something he never did before and likely will not do again. As soon as we had both the lantern and the table lamp burning we began our usual routine from an afternoon away. Daily chores.

I started the fire in the cook stove. Put water on to heat and change my clothes. Floyd was settling the horses in their stalls with fresh straw left there for them earlier. After unhitching them he stopped at the water trough for them to have a much needed drink.

As we finished our supper of canned homemade sausage and eggs both Fritz and Katrin seemed to have lots to tell us. Most of all they liked to talk about how they flew through the air. Fritz proudly said he did not even get a bloody nose. That must be something the boys at school talk about.

Before returning to the barn to finish chores, Floyd hugged them both telling them how proud he was of them. Most of all, he was so happy that no one was hurt. I had a few bruises as well as being a little sore, but nothing serious.

As I was doing my evening milking, I was determined that my mind would only drift to the good things that happen in the North. Oh yes, how could I have forgotten about Ira. On our way home Floyd and Gary Jenkins had relayed to me the story of Ira as told to them by Officer Judd, the town storyteller. They were mostly all true, perhaps a little extra added.

Ira is the young lad that had not returned home some months ago. His family said he had left for school but did not show up. None of his many siblings had any idea of his whereabouts but no one worried. He will show up. That seemed to be the way with the larger families.

One day after Christmas a scruffy looking man had stopped in at the blacksmith shop to purchase a poker. Jimmy did not know who he was. The strong smell of whiskey did not hide his bad odour along with the smell of smoke. He watched him as he headed north out of town on foot. His gut told him something was not just right. So he decided it would be best to have a talk with Officer Judd to see what he thinks.

Just before Jimmy closed his shop for the day, Officer Judd stopped by. Two other men had gone to the Jail House with similar reports that day.

One of the men was sure that it was Otis, the boot-legger. If it was, where was Rosco. Officer Judd thinks that he leaves his sidekick at home to guard his hootch.

Officer Judd had stopped in at the Red and White Store located not far from the Blacksmith Shop. Mr. Foster said he thought there was something unusual about his purchase. It was as though he had bought more than normal.

A few days later Officer Judd saddled his dark quarter horse Blaze and headed north from town. He had a good idea just where to look for this small shack that he knew was nestled in amongst the tall thick pine trees. He had ridden that way a few times to talk with the father of a couple young lads that enjoyed visiting town to have some fun. They always seemed to be in search of a poker game some place.

Blaze was just too happy to go for a good long run. As soon as they were out of town with no one in sight, he gave Blaze an almost free reign. They both enjoyed their quiet time as they galloped along as one with the cool fresh air in their faces.

As they neared the suspected area they slowed to a quiet trot looking for any sign of a footpath into the thick bush. Soon Officer Judd spotted their trail. Taking Blaze to a secluded spot near the path, he dismounted to proceed on foot. Otis had marked his path by breaking some of the branches for his customers. Otis was just too helpful.

He had not gone far when Rosco came to greet him showing off his big teeth. This was no surprise. He came prepared with plenty of treats in his pockets. Unlike Blaze, Rosco was always happy and hungry for something to eat taking whatever was offered.

As he neared the hut, through the trees he caught sight of some movement outside. Not sure if it was Otis or Ira, he drew his gun just in case. Otis has been known to randomly fire some warning shots in most any direction. Not being any too stable he was not one to see reasoning first. Officer Judd did not know the secret calling the customers used. He did not know if Ira too had a weapon or was even there.

With Rosco not wanting to leave the source of free treats, he made no effort to answer his masters' whistle. Otis was now becoming impatient and edgy. Would he do something impulsive? Maybe it is not Otis.

By now Officer Judd was close enough to see that the area in front of the hut was clear, he called out identifying himself. After repeating his call a couple times a young lad stepped out of the hut with his hands up.

"Hello, I am Officer Judd. What is your name?"

"Ira sir" he replied.

"I just stopped by for a visit with Otis. Is he here?"

"Nope."

"I will wait."

First making small talk about the owls that came out at night. He then had a one way discussion about the wild animals that were apt to wander through the trees. Just when he thought he may as well leave he hears the sound of a horse snorting as he came closer and closer. This could not be Blaze. He has been trained to not go with anyone else or eat anything that was not given to him by his partner. Perhaps it is a customer.

Out of the trail came Otis with Blaze following close behind. While Blaze slowly meandered along, he realized that Otis was humming his private tune with a big smile on his face. Now how did Otis learn that, it was just a made-up tune.

"Howrey Officher" Otis proudly stated. "I find yer horsch, Officher."

"Thanks Otis. That is right kind of you to lead him to me."

"Your hosch was loneschy."

"Otis, have you been drinking?"

"Yes shir."

"What have you been drinking?"

"Moooon Schine. Want shome Officher?"

"Now Otis, you know that stuff is against the law."

"Yes shir. Shh Shh. Don't tell shomebody."

Officer Judd said since he did not know how to proceed from there, he thought it would be a good idea to turn the attention to Ira who was sitting under a tree trying his best to stifle a grin. At least until he could think up a tactic that just might work with a very happy Otis who was still standing beside Blaze.

Since the attention was going to Ira, Otis decided it was time to have a conversation with Blaze whispering in his ear about the rabbit he has on the stove cooking. How he had found it in the bush looking real dead. Then Otis described in gory detail how he took his fur coat off 'im, pulled his innerds out and cut 'im up before the coyotes came along. He only been dead one night. Now Officer Judd began to wonder if Otis really did or is he just stringing a tall tale for Blaze.

After a few minutes it became obvious that Ira was not in the talking mood. So he decided to look around inside the hut. On the dirty stove sat a black pot coated on the outside with who knows what. On the inside doing a slow boil was something. After deciding that this was indeed the rabbit, at least judging by the shape of the legs, his stomach said lets get out of here and get some fresh air. Perhaps on another visit he will check out the pelts hanging on the walls.

Trying once more to talk to Ira, he thought he would ask him about his family, and was it not time to return home to help on the farm. Nope, came the sharp reply. It seems that the only word in his vocabulary was nope. At least the only word he was willing to part with. Since he appeared to be in his middle teens Officer Judd knew there was no way he could be forced to return. He would just leave again. His feeling was that perhaps his parents were relieved they now had one less mouth to feed.

"Otis, what are you going to do with that Moon Shine?"

"Give'd it to yer horsch."

"Now Otis, no need to be a dumb bumb. I know you did not. Horses only drink water."

"Not yer horsch."

Having had enough of Otis's big smile he thought he would just leave as soon as he gave them both some strong words about breaking the law, and how he did not really want to put them in jail.

As he rode along the lonely road he thought how this might be a good time to visit with Ira's family for a couple minutes.

Upon his arrival a half dozen young children all-talking at once surrounded him. Before he could dismount, a robust lady with long dark hair came out of the slab home that really was nothing more than a shack leaning heavily to one side. She wore an old washed out blue dress showing many years of wear and well-worn gumboots. She quickly stated that her husband was working in the far field, and I should state my business and move on. I thought, so much for being afraid of the law.

It was easy to see that this lady with only two teeth at the front was heavy with child so thought it best to just state my business and move on like she said. As briefly as I could, I told her what I knew of Ira. I asked her if she wanted him home. Much to my shock her instant reply was NOPE, loud and clear.

"Well, has he been giving you trouble?" I asked.

"Nope, just time for him to move on."

Now I just had to ask one more question. "So how many babies have you had?"

"I have fourteen babies, and I love 'em all," she said. With that I bid her farewell with a tip of my hat and as warm a smile as I could muster, Blaze and I headed back to town.

Chapter Forty-Two

Fall was quickly approaching and still no word from Klaus. With each passing day I began to feel a little more despondent. Could it possibly be that he will not come? The biggest news in town has been that the war has ended, our soldiers have been returning home. My brother Clyde will be among those returning, should he have survived this terrible nightmare. I had no way of knowing.

As I emptied the bathtub of its now cool water onto the dry dusty ground in front of our house, I thought of how many times my family and I took our weekly bath outside in the yard. It was much easier than emptying it from inside. Today the air was feeling too cool for this, but it was what I hoped would be my last bath in the outdoors.

The flies had left the house until spring, which meant the air was too cold for them. There were still some hanging around the animals in the barn. I am sure the poor cows and horses must be tired of having to keep their tails swishing back and forth to find relief from these pesky creatures. It is now time to take the fly strips down from inside the house and burn them. It seems the mosquitoes have left with their friends. They will both return next year.

School began two weeks ago. Sunday afternoon there will be a social gathering at the Little School House. The men and older boys will play a game of softball. After they tire out everyone will gather around on the grassy field for a visit. Time to catch up on what the teacher has planned for the year, and anything else that anyone may feel needs to be shared. We were happy this was planned on our non-church Sunday.

For the past year, we have been fortunate to have a Lutheran Pastor hold services at the school in the next community. This was a more reasonable drive with horses, only four and a half miles each way. While this was only possible every other week, we welcomed him with open arms. Unfortunately his services were in German. None of the children could speak or understand more than a few words. No one had any children's books for them to read so we just hoped that with listening, which they did not always do, they would learn a little.

By the time we arrived for church we were all dusty from travel. This followed by an inspection of my children before they climbed out of our wagon. Usually a spit wash was needed. They hated it. Fritz complained bitterly.

Floyd would tie up the horses in the open shelter along with the other teams. This was just a place to keep the sun off them in the summer and the snow in the winter. There was only one team that did not like the presence of others nearby so they were tied up a little further away to the lone pine tree.

Harvesting season was coming to a close. I had most of the garden reaped, canned and stored in the cellar. Sauerkraut was yet to be made. The butchering was done. Sausages were made and canned. The chickens were canned in the cellar waiting to be enjoyed for Sunday dinners. Floyd still had fieldwork to do before the snow came, but he too was nearly ready.

Two weeks later I was outside taking the clothes off the line that I had washed earlier that morning when I heard the sound of a car coming closer and closer. This was not the time for company. My hair was bundled on top of my head with a babushka knotted on top. I wore my only pair of farm boots; half worn out black gumboots that had seen many trips to the barnyard. Instead of wearing my work dress today, I decided I would wear Floyd's extra pair of overalls. They would be washed tomorrow anyway. I knew I looked a sight but there was no one around, not even my family.

I ran inside the house as quickly as I could but I was no match for a 1943 Black Ford Coupe with a crazy driver leaning on the horn. Another man was leaning out his window waving and calling. As the car circled around the back of the house stopping at the door, doors flew open and out jumped three people I could barely recognize. The tears began to stream down my cheeks as I ran towards them. For now I forgot how I looked.

Clyde came with two cousins. Bernard and his younger sister Muriel. I was not expecting Clyde, only Klaus. For the next moments I was so over-joyed with surprise I was not in any way disap-pointed. I had always loved Clyde too. He was just more serious than Klaus. He did not know of my plans. So I thought anyway.

After excusing myself to change my clothes I

left them to wander around. When I went back outside they were standing there beside the door with the laundry on their arms all neatly folded. No one had done such a kind deed for me since I had left home. Once again I was overwhelmed.

Clyde was still the same guy with dark bushy curly hair and his usual sturdy build. I thought he was a little more carefree than I remembered. He was no longer the quiet reserved brother that seldom had anything to say. I thought he was just about perfect, not too loud, and not too quiet.

Muriel had been taking her last years of high school when we left. Now she was a working lady, and a beautiful one with dark brown eyes that sparkled as she spoke. Her maturity had blossomed. She spoke with confidence in a kind and caring manner.

Then there was Bernard. One could not miss that broad smile that seemed to cover his face. I could see that he was still as full of mischief as ever. He had been the most outgoing of the Ziegler family. For certain, that had not changed. This visit would not be dull.

Bernard and Muriel said they would go to the field in search of their cousin they had not seen for some time. As soon as they were out of hearing, Clyde told me of how he could help my children and I escape from the barren North. He understood that we will need to talk privately as no one else knew of the plans him and Klaus had made.

With both Floyd and I having so many siblings it would be a long visit to have us both informed as to all the happenings in Estuary. As I began to make coffee Clyde kept assuring me life was only going to get better. Being the family planner, he said he had it all planned out. Do not worry. This was much easier for him to say than for me to feel. I promised I would try.

Klaus had met a red haired lady, fell in love and moved away from Estuary. They now have a little girl born in 1940 who was the apple of her mother's eye. She could do no wrong. It did not appear that Clyde thought so too. Klaus was happy and healthy living just far enough away to be on his own but able to return a couple times a year.

Soon all five of us were sitting down enjoying coffee as we happily chatted away. As we only had four chairs, one person had to sit on a bed. They insisted they did not mind. What were they to do? I was still looking at Clyde with wonder as to how he had survived the war as well as he had. It was quickly obvious that he had a hearing problem. Details will come later.

As my mind began to linger on what I was going to feed three more people that had travelled so many miles, it suddenly came to my mind that was the least of my worries. I had a bigger problem. Where were they going to sleep? There was only one bed each with one blanket for each bed. Neither Fritz or Katrin had a pillow. Once again I quickly offered up a silent prayer to God to help me through these few days. Still I wondered how I would manage. Then I remembered that we also only had four plates etc. We could not all eat at the same time.

As though reading my mind, Clyde suggested him and I go outside to see if the kinner are walking along the road. I knew this meant he had something private to say. I will need to be alert for any ways he had for us to speak without questioning him.

The first thing he said was not to worry about sleeping. When we are alone we will discuss his plans. I was so relieved I wanted to cry, not put on a brave happy face.

By the time we were nearing the barnyard I could see them leaving the road to our farm. I had not mentioned a word to anyone of this impending visit, so there was much surprise for everyone including Floyd. As for him, I felt a sudden hope that Muriel would be able to convince him to leave this barren land.

They were both happy to see a real live Uncle that had come to visit that was full of smiles and hugs. Upon finding these people were going to stay for a couple days, they both drew closer to each other with a bewildered look on their faces. I knew it was beds, where will we sleep?

When we came to the front of the house, they both stopped with eyes wide open. Finally Katrin said, "Fritz, its a car."

"Woweee! Does it run?"

As Clyde opened the door he told them they could go inside it and have a look around. Then their greatest surprise, Clyde promised them he would help each of them take it for a drive. They were so happy you would have thought they were just given a trip to the moon and back.

Soon it was time to remind them they needed to do their chores before dinner. Bernard said he would help them. He would split the wood and help carry it in. Muriel said she would help Katrin with the chickens. Clyde would help with the milking. First Fritz and Katrin would need to bring the cows in from where they were lazily grazing in the pasture.

I was so relieved to find that they had visited Mr. Bosch on their way through town where they were able to receive direction to the one and only butcher. I did not care what kind of meat it was; it would be a big treat. Just before going to the well to lower his purchases into the cold water, he whispered that he brought bologna for their lunch tomorrow. I could have cried. A treat they had never tasted.

Everyone worked fast and hard so time could be spent together enjoying each other's company. When dinner was ready, Clyde and Bernard said they had more chairs. How could that be? In minutes they returned each carrying a block of wood, their chairs.

Clyde insisted his little niece would sit on his knee sharing his plate. Muriel said she would love to share with Fritz since she now had a young cousin to get to know. That still left us one plate short. With that Bernard insisted he could use the lid off a pot.

In embarrassment and shame, I could no longer hold back my tears. I still had to tell them there were only four forks and four knives. We did have a few spoons. They each did their best to assure me that we can manage for a few days. This was no trouble.

When the evening chores were finished we had a chance to sit around and catch up on our missing lives with each other. Bernard told Floyd how he was helping his father with the farm. There would be room for him to marry and settle on the farm with a family of his own. Having been busy helping on the farm as well as helping others while their sons were away serving in the War, he had not met anyone as yet. Muriel assured us she would help find a brave lady that was strong enough to live with a crazy man.

Clyde did not wish to speak of his time serving away from home other than to say that he will never get over breathing in the smell of the trenches or the sights of his fallen companions. Perhaps one day he will be able to sleep without the sound of war ringing in his ears. He may have been suffering from what is known today as PTSD, Post Traumatic Stress Disorder. For now we will enjoy each other. Time to catch up on family.

Much too soon it was time for Fritz and Katrin to go to bed. There was school tomorrow. Now I wondered where everyone would sleep. We only have three beds. Two are single cots with no pillows. Each bed had one blanket each. As I started to say something, Bernard said no time to fret. We had this sorted out before we left home.

Without further ado, him and Clyde said they were going out to build themselves a bed of straw in the barn before it got too late. They had brought with them a lantern and three blankets. They would not be cold. I wondered what the danger of coyotes would be. Would they try to break their way into the barn in one of the weak areas? Floyd assured me they would stay in the middle of the barn and off the floor. Their scent would not so easily be picked up.

Fritz wanted to sleep in the barn too but with school the next day, we said no. As a surprise I agreed to that for their last night with us. Muriel and Katrin would share her cot. While Katrin was excited about this, I knew she did not know how tight it would be. Tight it was. Poor Muriel, but what were we to do.

The next day they decided we should make the sauerkraut. That was a big job that took not nearly as much time with the extra helping hands. What fun we had, laughing and story telling. Before I knew it the chores were done, sauerkraut made and time left to visit before dinner.

The next two days we kept the kinner home from school for family time. We went for rides in the car exploring the scenic North. They wanted to see each and every thing there was. They said how much they enjoyed the area but it was not anything like they had thought it would be. It was much more desolate.

Little by little during our evening visit, Clyde began reminiscing of his time overseas fighting

with the allies. He told of the many atrocities the
German forces imposed on the Jewish people. We
then spoke of our dear friends, Mr. and Mrs. Hister.
They lived on the farm next to our family in Estuary. They were not only our closest neighbours but
our dearest friends. They were Jews. After listening
to Clyde tell of this horror story, we decided that
we would no longer speak German in our home or
out of it. We were too ashamed.

While Clyde and I had managed some time alone
to discuss my desire to leave the North, it was all
too soon for them to prepare to leave in the morning. Clyde spent extra time in the evening playing
with the children. He magically pulled more treats
from his pockets earning him even more hugs. Before going to bed, he slipped me one more surprise.
This one was private and special.

That night as we slept, Mother Nature had a
surprise of her own for us. We woke in the morning
to two feet of snow and still coming down in heavy
large white flakes. The wind was blowing fiercely.
The snow banks were building. There would not be
any travelling today.

By noon the sun began to shine, the snow was
no longer falling, the cold wind had dissipated,
there was now a gentle breeze leaving a cold feel to
the air. With Buck's help they would break a road
out to the main road. First the car had to be pulled
out of the mound of snow covering it.

By the time it was time to do chores again,
they were all set to leave in the morning. They
laughed and joked about how much they would

need to shovel and push in the next couple days. Muriel and I had baked bread so they would have fresh bread to take with them today. Well, tomorrow it would be one day old.

Chapter Forty-Three

It is now a year since Clyde visited. I spent that winter worrying about the children getting to and from school. We no longer had a teacher. There was not a grade eight student willing to take on keeping the students in order. It was much too big a job for a fourteen year old as well as keeping up their studies by mail order. The students had already taken the previous year by mail order while at school. The school must be shut down.

Fritz and Katrin would now have to walk to the next community school. With climbing over fences, walking through the fields, it would be a three-mile walk each way. They would get up, eat their breakfast and leave. They were still in elementary school. While I insisted they go if there was no blizzard, as soon as I was alone I would shed many tears of worry.

I worried that the coyotes would be out prowling before they reached home. I knew that some days there were bears in the fields. Each night and all day I prayed that God would watch over them.

There was a saying amongst the women, make-do-and-mend. And mend I did. I mended all Floyd's socks and pants as well as the socks for the children. I rummaged through the box of clothes my sister had sent, remaking clothes for Katrin and I.

I made over a dress for myself. It had a peter-pan collar with a flowered A-line skirt. Then I tucked it away where it would be out of sight. I was so grateful for the extra threads she had tucked inside her parcel for me to sew with. Next I made over a blue dress for Katrin. I found a plaid skirt in the box to make over for her as well. There was a dark blue coat for Katrin with a brooch pinned on the front in a light grey colour with two birds sitting on a nest. She will love it. I will just need to remove it from my hiding place and hem it next winter. There were more than enough clothes in the box for Fritz.

I unravelled old sweaters to make up new ones. I knit as often as I could find the time. There was a nice sweater for Floyd that I would save for next winter. Time was running out to get him to change his mind, but not looking hopeful.

I planted even a larger garden this year than ever before. Each and every Mason Jar would be filled with vegetables, sausages and chickens. While the winter was filled with cold winds and snow, the spring came with sunshine and warmth.

I worked long days pulling the weeds in the garden to prevent them from suffocating the vegetable plants. I kept the potatoes hilled to protect them from unwanted insects and the bright sunshine that would turn each potato green should it reach them.

I cherished each and every visit with the Faust family. Bertha had become my dearest friend and confidant. After each chat as we looked at the flowers growing in our gardens, we shared a look of understanding for each other. One that said this would all come to an end. Many a time we would part with tears falling that we would not explain. Not to anyone.

The children had made new friends at school. They were happy to find that Miss Beulah was their teacher. Now they needed to get used to calling her, Mrs. West. This was the school that both Carmen and Grace attended so they went there aware that there would be someone they knew.

Each and every day I listened for the sound of the Indian ponies pulling their wagon along our rutted road. There was none. I spoke to Mr. Bosch each time I went to town. It seemed that Chief Barefoot had led his tribe to a different land. The new Chief did not know of Chief Barefoot or did not understand. Chances of my seeing Amitola again were becoming more distant.

One sunny day I had the laundry hanging on the clothesline to dry with the gentle breeze swinging the sheets back and forth. With the door open leaving the screen door to prevent a few flies from entering, I swept and scrubbed to clean our home. All of a sudden I heard Fritz and Katrin shouting as they came running to the house, "Momma, Momma, the Preacher's Coming." Like every time they came, I looked a sight. My heart would sink and my stomach would rise. Those were the words I dreaded to hear them shout the most. By the time Floyd reached the house, the Preacher and family had driven to the front in their shiny black car. If only just once they would visit when we were not in our old work clothes looking like the poor church mice that we were. At least we were not outside bathing in our dented tub while the sun shone down on us trying to keep us warm. I think that is what my father meant when he would say there is always a good side to everything.

Reverend Ludwig was a plump man of average height with a booming voice. His thick dark brown hair had a wind-blown look due to its' coarse wiry texture. His moustache and long eyebrows were the same. His front missing tooth was hardly noticeable any more. His quick friendly smile made him instantly liked.

However, Mrs. Ludwig did not so quickly endure the congregation to her. She was a slim stately woman who looked ten years younger than her age of close to the middle forties. She was never seen without her black wide brimmed hat with a red band accenting a large red feather that quite became her tall slim stature. Even with her black handbag over her arm, and wearing plush black gloves she walked with an elegance befitting the lady she portrayed. She had a beautiful smile but was rarely seen. It was clear she felt these visits a duty only. One she must endure.

Their two young daughters were also dressed in lovely blue coats over ivory dresses with smocked tops and plain skirts, but never a smile showing. When prompted by their father they would each give a polite hello but nothing more. I knew both Katrin and Fritz were hurt by the way they were looked down upon. Their good manners and smiles made us proud but did little to ease their pain of being so poor.

After sending my children to play, our guests were invited inside for a cup of coffee. I no longer bothered to remind them of the sticky fly strips hanging from the ceiling lest one would catch her shiny red feather. Each time after she had sat down I could see her eyes go to the fly strips in horror. I just smiled. Their visit always seemed to be the day before I baked bread and so all I could offer was coffee and milk for their daughters to which they always shook their heads from one side to the other. They apparently had not been taught to answer when spoken to.

After a short while of idle conversation, Reverend Ludwig read a couple passages from his bible, offered a prayer and said they must be on their way. This was my queue to give them some food for coming to visit us unannounced and not really wanted.

When I called Fritz and Katrin to come to say good-bye, I asked Fritz to climb down into the cellar to bring up a sealer of home made sausage to give. This would have meant two meals for us. Whether they ate it, appreciated it or disliked it I never knew but it was the best we could do.

As soon as they left we all began our chores. Laundry needed to be brought in from the clothesline. Sheets put back on the beds for the night. Milking needed to be done before making dinner. This would be the night for biscuits and eggs. There was a small jar of canned pickled pigs feet I would open for a treat with the biscuits. Floyd said he had something to say about the visit today as

soon as we were finished eating. This encouraged
Fritz and Katrin to fill the wood box and coal bin
before supper so they wouldn't have to hurry outside. Floyd began by telling Fritz and Katrin how
proud he was of the way they behaved earlier today. "The Ludwig girls may have fancier clothes
but they have no manners," he would say. "They
are two spoiled girls that like to whine more than
anything else. Remember when they came to visit
us last year early in the spring?" With that we all
laughed. How could we ever forget.

Chapter Forty-Four

It was early spring. Most of the snow had melted. It rained heavily most of day pounding the ground with a torrential downpour mixed with hail. By the time we went to bed the rain had let up to where it was just considered heavy rain mixed with showers throughout the morning hours. By noon our road was a muddy mess. Wearing gumboots was a must. The ditches were overflowing leaving the banks soft and slippery. The cattails were shooting up along the banks of the deep ditches soon to show off their furry brown heads.

By noon the bright prairie sun was shinning down warming the dirt roads to a deep soft mud. It was much too treacherous to be driving. A horse could easily slip and fall, the wagon wheel could so easily slide off the road landing into the ditch overrun with water. The farmers all stayed home spending their time working around their farms. There was much to be done after a rain storm.

It was mid afternoon when Fritz and Katrin came running to the house shouting "Momma, Momma, the Preacher's Coming." How could that be, I wondered. I had not heard a car. Then Katrin came running in again laughing. "Momma, daddy wants you to come to the corral. Hurry." With that she turned and ran back out before I could ask what was going on. What ever could be happening that is so funny.

When I arrived at the corral wearing my gumboots with my old work dress I had to struggle to keep the smile off my face too. There stood Reverend Ludwig in mud covering his shiny dress shoes and pants. He clearly had slipped and fallen landing on his backside.

"See Momma, the Reverend fell in the mud and got his pants dirty," said Katrin not even trying to hide the smile from her face.

Before I could say anything more, I heard a giggle from Fritz so I felt compelled to remind them that we must not laugh at others. I looked over at Floyd to help me out only to find him standing there leaning on a shovel with a huge smile on his face. By the time he attempted to cover his face with his hand, it was too late. The Reverend had seen. With that he burst out laughing leaving everyone free to join in. Reverend Ludwig was laughing the hardest.

"So Reverend, what happened and where is your car?" asked Floyd as he tried to be serious.

"Well you see, we were driving along when the girls began to squabble in the back seat. Their mother to no avail had scolded them several times today. I turned around to scold them when a wheel caught into a rut. I pulled too hard on the steering wheel over compensating to where I was now too close to the edge of the road sliding in the soft earth to the ditch. With three females screaming in my ear I too panicked."

"Is everyone out of the car?" asked Floyd.

"Haa, no I mean, stuttered the Reverend. The Mrs. is afraid she will ruin her shoes, the girls too. I told them they all had to sit on the high side of the

car to keep it from rolling over which then turned
into near hysteria," said the Reverend with a mis-
chievous chuckle in his voice. "It is only the one
back wheel that is stuck in the lower side of the
ditch, but I fear there might be more damage as
the back wheels do not turn as I give the engine
more gas. It will keep the girls still."

"O.K. Fritz, let's hitch our team and see if we
can pull them out," said Floyd with ease as though
this was something they did every week.

As Katrin and I walked back to the house my
thoughts went to what I was going to feed them
for supper. As Katrin carried in more wood for the
stove I made sure the house was as tidy as possible.
Then Katrin and I went to the chicken house to
gather the eggs. With each step I wished that there
would be more eggs than usual. There was not. I
will give them the seven that we gathered and hope
they will not break them before arriving home. I
did not ask Katrin to go to the cellar to bring up
potatoes and vegetables as I was afraid they would
take that as an invitation to stay for supper. I will
tend to that later.

Soon I heard our team clopping along on our
road as they neared the corral with a dirty city car
limping behind. Once again I put my gumboots
back on and headed out to the barn. No matter
how much I wished, our muddy yard had not instantly dried up. How would Mrs. Ludwig and her
dainty girls handle this? There was only one pair
of gumboots for each of us. We had no extras.
Somehow I could not picture her or her daughters

in muddy gumboots but the thought brought a smile to my face.

When I got closer I heard Fritz say to the girls, "well, ya gettin out?"

They both just stared at him like they could not believe what they had just heard. Floyd having lost his usual passive face in time of need was now hiding behind his sleeve as though he was wiping his face. I knew him better than that. It seemed it was up to me to step in and suggest something.

I thought it would be a good time for Mrs. Ludwig and the girls to come to the house to sit while the men decided what was to be done with the car. Now how to get them there was going to take some imagination.

As we all stood there looking at her, Katrin said "do you want to ride on Misty to the house? Momma rides her all the time. She won't bite you. She won't kick you if you don't stand behind her."

I am sure at the same moment both Floyd and I pictured this prim lady with dress and hat being helped atop a horse, there did not seem to be a way of glossing this over.

Giving poor Katrin, who was only trying to help, a stern look as she replied, "Never! I shall not sit on a smelly horse."

Reverend Ludwig cast Katrin a smile that had great idea written all over it, but instead suggested to his wife that he would carry her. While she stood there trying to decide if that would be ok, he grabbed her around her thighs and threw her over his shoulder. With her arms dangling down his back, she watched as her treasured hat fell to the ground landing in the mud. With his big smile still on his face, he patted her on her bottom and strode off to the house. This sent Floyd and both children into a fit of muffled laughter.

I reached the house just in time to open the door for our special guests. I couldn't help but wonder if God was watching his servant now. I am sure He too would be smiling. As he set his wife down as carefully as a piece of fine china, he quickly brushed a kiss across her check.

"I will be right back with our daughters," he said as he turned and left not waiting for a reply.

True to his word, he soon returned with two frowning girls each clinging to an arm, as they both whined "don't drop me in the mud papa." In true fatherly fashion, "next time you whine and squirm I will. Just see if I won't," he said. With that he turned and headed back to the corral.

I quickly put a pot of water on the hottest part of the stove for coffee and cocoa for the four children. I was almost afraid to look in the Fry's cocoa tin for fear it would be nearly empty. Please let there be four spoonfuls I silently prayed.

Now I was left to make conversation with a stern lady who depended on her husband to speak for their family. I was fully aware that she had no knowledge or desire to have knowledge of farm life. In all the times they visited us not once did she even glance toward the field or garden area. Both girls were standing beside their mother as stiff as two soldiers. When I suggested they might like to sit, they both stared at me as though I spoke a foreign language. Oh how I had to bite my tongue, but I knew this visit was just beginning.

With my most patient voice and gentlest smile I spoke first vowing to make the most of this difficult day for four city people.

Soon the men and my children came inside to render the news. Close inspection had determined the rear universal joint had broken and the drive shaft was laying on the ground. The car was not driveable. Floyd could fix most any piece of farm equipment but this was beyond his capability. Now what? Their car was broken. It was late in the afternoon. What were we to do with the Reverend and his family? Nothing to do but feed them, find a place for them to bed for the night.

Floyd suggested come morning, he would tie the drive shaft up with barbwire under the car to keep it from further damage. With using the horses tow the car to town where the local mechanic could make the necessary repairs. Reverend and his family could ride in the car while it was being towed. There was nothing to do but make the best of it.

I knew that they would at the very least be staying for dinner. So I set about peeling potatoes, carrots and a turnip. I pulled the meat pail up from the well, removed a couple larger pieces of pork to roast in the oven. I decided to splurge and chop a whole onion to add to the meat.

The children and I filled the wood box, the coal bin and then tended to the chickens. Katrin gathered the eggs while Fritz sprinkled some food for them. It was a little early to milk the cows but company or no company it will need to be done later. For now we will fill the water trough for the animals. Together Fritz and Katrin could carry the slop pail from the house to the pig pen, empty it in their trough, wash it out at the well and put it back into the house. We put fresh straw in the stalls for Buck and Misty. We were all getting tired but we needed to bring the cows in from the pasture before taking a much-needed break.

When I called them all in to dinner I explained that their family would eat first. It was obvious even to Mrs. Ludwig there was only four chairs. When the Reverend started to insist we eat with them, I then had to explain that we did not have enough dishes. For the first time, Mrs. Ludwig showed a sign of compassion. With one firm look at her daughters she said they would eat with Fritz and Katrin.

While we adults ate, my children showed the girls the game of String and how to play it. They had never seen such a thing. Soon they each wanted a turn. It took a few minutes for them to get the big red button to spin on a circle of string that was wound up tight as elastic. They were elated begging their papa to make them one when they got home for their house.

Later while I was milking the cows, Floyd came over to talk to me. In a low voice he said the Ludwig's would need to spend the night with us. I was not surprised but a huge knot did form in the pit of my stomach. There were three beds three with three blankets and eight people. Oh Floyd, is there room in our Inn?

When I came in from milking, Mrs. Ludwig had finished washing up the dishes from the children. The table was wiped and the floor swept. I was so grateful I wanted to hug her instead of just saying "thank you very much. That is a big help."

"You have gone out of your way for us, it is the least I can do. You made us a delicious dinner. Thank you. I am sorry we imposed on you."

When the men came in Reverend said they had been talking. We will need to beg your forgiveness for this intrusion. My family and I will spend the night in the barn in the extra stall. There is straw we can use.

Now Mrs. Ludwig had just lost her composure. I knew she was grateful for our help but sleeping in a barn in their day clothes? That really was not fitting a lady. As the water began to surface in her eyes, Floyd spoke up.

"No, no Reverend, stop teasing her. We decided that Fritz and us two men will sleep in the barn. Mrs. Ludwig can sleep in Fritz's bed, the girls in Katrin's bed and Katrin can sleep with her momma. Will that be ok with you Emma?"

"Yes, that will work. If Mary and Joseph could manage when the Inn was full, we can manage with a small house and a stable. Everyone will be warm."

What will they think when they find I have no change of sheets? Thought Emma.

That evening instead of my telling my children

a Bible story, I asked Mrs. Ludwig if she would tell a story to them before they said their nighttime prayers. She was delighted. What a great story- teller she was. My children and I were mesmerized. We hung on to each and every word. By the time she finished all four children were laughing togeth- er as they became friends. Two different worlds were coming together in friendship.

Then we were treated to a impromptu minia- ture service by Reverend Ludwig. His message of how we help others in need; how we need to be appreciative of those lending a helping hand with whatever they have to share touched each of us in a way I shall never forget. That man does have a timely way with words.

As Floyd stood up he spoke a farmer's famous words, "Well, morning comes early. We must all go to bed." With that we bid each other good night and headed for our beds eager to lay our tired bod- ies down to rest.

It was during the night that I heard a noise. It was Mrs. Ludwig. The next morning she told me how she had woken with a very strong need to use the bathroom. Thinking that with the clear night sky she would find her way with only the light of the moon. She carefully let herself out trying not to waken me. She walked in the stillness of the night nearing the bush where the outhouse was to be found. Just as she stepped into the path, there was a loud howl from within the bush area. She stopped in her tracks afraid to go any further. With her heart pounding loudly and another howl ringing in her ears, she turned running as fast as she could for the house.

This did not solve her problem. She decided she would just have to squat beside the house but now she had no paper. The Eaton's Catalogue was in the outhouse. She would have to make do with a few leaves. No one will know. She could be back inside and into bed in another few minutes. She would not be missed.

Just as she got herself settled, she saw something moving silently across the ground in her direction. Before she could stop herself, she had let out one blood-curdling scream that not only woke me but Floyd as well. We were both trained to listen for any noise in the night lest it be an intruder with four feet.

While I had no light, I felt I must go and see what happened. By the time I was there, Floyd was coming with the lantern as fast as he could run in the night. I didn't have to ask what had happened. I just led her back into the house telling Floyd all was well. He could go back to sleep. When we were safely inside, she apologized profusely for yet another disruption. I assured her that it was no problem. With that we both climbed into our beds hoping to get some more sleep before daylight. Next time I think she will be more willing to use the chamber pot. The enamel may have a few chips, but when the need arises in the night, it doesn't matter.

When morning came, I quickly stoked the fire in preparation for making breakfast, hot cooked oatmeal porridge. I heard a soft good morning, Emma. To my surprise there was Mrs. Ludwig climbing out of her bed in a very wrinkled fancy dress. In her bare feet she padded over to me, gave me a hug as she said "please, call me Helga." I knew then that this stern lady with a soft heart beneath would become my friend. "Tell me what you do and I will try to make it half as good as yours while you do your outside chores."

As I neared the corral there was Reverend trying to wash his black dress shoe off. With a sheepish smile he said that they didn't have cow pies in the city and laughed some more. He was truly enjoying this farm experience. His shoes were so caked with mud I am surprised he could tell. He doesn't know it yet but they will smell real good in a while.

As the men ate their porridge, they talked of how they would prepare the car to be towed. Floyd was anxious to get started, as it would be a long day before he would return.

As Helga and I cleared up the dishes her girls played inside as my children went about doing their chores. Like most children they got to chasing each other around in our small space until, just as Helga told them, something will get knocked over. Sure enough, there went the slop pail covering Helga's shoes and splashing her stockings with a watery mess of left over food and wash water waiting to be taken to the pigpen. This was another great reason to sit and cry.

It was mid morning when the men returned to the house ready for a cup of coffee before they left for town. They stopped off at the well to wash but Reverend still looked a sight for sore eyes. Just as I was about to say coffee would only be a couple minutes, we heard a shocked voice say, "Papa, you are a dirty mess." Not daring to say anything, we tried to keep the smiles from our faces so as to not embarrass him. Much to my surprise Helga was the first to start to laugh with everyone joining in.

A short while later I was saying good-bye to our unexpected guests. This was truly a blessing in disguise. We got to know them as ordinary people. They got to know us as fellow Christians, not just poor farmers. While words were not spoken, I knew they had come to understand our difficult life having a better appreciation for all members of their congregation. With watery eyes, Helga hugged me as she thanked us for our kindness. Then she said just what I wasn't sure I wanted to hear, "I am so looking forward to our next visit."

Floyd had the team harnessed up and in front of the car. Towrope was fastened to the front axle and all was made ready to go. Reverend and family piled in. Floyd would ride on the back of a horse in order to guide them on their way. Off they went to town and Joe's Garage.

As soon as they were on their way Fritz started to laugh. "Hey mom, that was so funny when Reverend walked behind Buck just as Buck let off some real smelly gas."

"For sure. Bad timing," she chuckled too. "This must be our family secret."

On his return, Floyd told of the uneventful trip

and the Reverends good fortune on reaching town. Turned out Joe was a member of the local Lutheran Church and was more than willing to accommodate the Reverend and his family with room and board until such time as he could have the car fixed. God's good fortune surely shone on the Reverend this day.

Chapter Forty-Five

With the Little School House having closed, we missed the community gatherings. There had not been a Christmas Concert or a Social where we had the opportunity to visit with those we had come to know as friends. It was another reminder of how barren it was.

Just after seeding time two neighbouring farmers decided we should have a ball game at the Little School House. They set a date, mounted their horses and rode off to spread the word. One covered the West side of the community; the other covered the East side. When the day arrived the turnout was overwhelming. Everyone was eager to play.

The young children ran around chasing each other in a game of tag, some chose to play on their favourite swing, the ladies sat on the ground cheering on the players as they inquired as to the well-being of their families. The men and older boys had a great time as they ran around their cow-pie bases cheering their team on. When they were too tired to run anymore, it was time to bid everyone a cheerful farewell.

Before we all left, Clara and Walter had an announcement. Their oldest daughter Jean is planning to marry just before harvesting. She told how Roy is a nice young man but a little older. He lives East of town on his father's farm.

When Roy was seventeen his mother passed away during childbirth. His father had gone into a deep depression leaving Roy with the care of his father as well as two younger brothers. The farm had now been signed over to him. His brothers would stay on for a while yet and help out. Then they would search for work elsewhere.

They were going to have a town preacher come to their farm to officiate. They would then serve a lunch outside in their yard. Floyd was asked to bring his fiddle. Norman offered to bring his banjo. Will had a mouth organ that he would bring and play. Walter wants for us to have a real shindig, as Jean just loves to dance, Clara explained. She will be the happiest when her and Roy are kicking up their heels in time to the music.

The ladies all offered to bring something to add to her lunch. I didn't know what I would bring, but knew I could think up something.

Just as I feared, one sunny day a car came rolling into our yard. I knew by the sound that it was the Ludwig family. For the first time I greeted them with a sincere smile and a warm welcome. Helga was out of the car before it came to a full stop with her arms wide open for a hug. I felt so much friendship in this greeting that I had never felt before. Oh my, she wore no hat. Umm! She wore a nice dress in a soft green making her look not nearly so uppity and stern. Their girls were dressed in print dresses of blue that made them look as though they were ready to play, and play they did.

By now Reverend had gone to the field to find Floyd. As I invited Helga to come into the house she reached back inside the car and removed a box.

"Emma, I baked some cookies for our coffee

time together. I cannot bake bread or anything with dough. I have heard that your bread is the best in the community. I couldn't wait to come back to see you. Please forgive me for being a not very good Christian. You have taught me well."

"Helga, all is well. Let us be friends and enjoy this. How did you know I miss cookies so much? Yesterday I baked bread. You shall take a loaf home for your breakfast tomorrow."

After a short visit and some delicious cookies, they said they needed to leave. Once again their girls whined. This time it was because they had to leave, they were having too much fun.

I thought back to our afternoon as I was milking. I knew this was a lady that I would fondly remember for always.

There were only two sisters that were able to have a horse to ride to town in order to continue their education. For the rest it was mail order studies or nothing. I began to think of Fritz going into grade seven next week, his last year of studies. Katrin would then need to walk this long distance to the next community by herself. I was sure that Floyd would not allow an eleven-year-old girl to do that, especially his daughter. If I was going to see Fritz become a farmer, I did not want it to be this far north. I knew that in a couple short years he would become a Hobo travelling to where he could beg someone to give him work. I knew it was not in his heart to be a bum begging someone for help with work in return. Until then he would be working on our farm. I want better for my children.

Fritz had already mentioned to me several times that while helping his dad in the fields Floyd had said to him that next year he will not have to go to school. He would be spending all his time being a farmer working in the fields from morning until evening. I felt that when Fritz was with me he wanted to go to school but while he was with his dad he would agree to just working in the fields. He was too young to be doing a man's work.

I savoured each moment of the good parts of our life. There was the forest of large green pine trees, the soft silvery birch trees, the sweet smell of the wild berries, and the hot summer sun. There was the beautiful vast prairie sky that seemed to never end. The clear nights where I could look up and see the man in the moon. The warm friendships I have enjoyed with the ladies even though they were much too far apart. My quiet time with Misty and Bossy. They were always willing to listen as I poured my heart out in troubled times. Sometimes I sang as they patiently listened comforting me. I never though for a second that my best companion on a farm would be a cow.

Winter was well under way once again. The snow deep, the air cold and the wind blew. I convinced Floyd that come Sunday we should hitch the team to our sleigh and visit the Faust family. I needed a visit with a human friend.

When Sunday came we woke to a beautiful sunny day, perfect for a sleigh ride. I was so happy that I sang all the way with Floyd and the children chiming in many times. A couple times Floyd commented that I was so happy it was worth the long trip.

Much to my surprise as soon as Bertha and I were alone in the house she said she had a surprise for me. From her apron pocket she removed a sheet of paper. She had received a letter for me from my sister Ursula as well as some money. It was for my ticket out.

"Oh Bertha. However did she find your address?" I was confused and dizzy with happiness. I could barely think.

"When Clyde was here, he asked for it but not to tell you. The wait may have been too much for you to bear in silence. I will miss you and the children but know that it is for the best. We will be leaving this northland in the next year or two as well. Marvin said he would not say anything to Floyd. We must do what we have to do for our children. We will watch out for Floyd until he adjusts to his knew life. Maybe then he will change his mind. I will give you a piece of paper and a pencil that you can write your reply. I will mail it for you."

"The next time the train will come will be December 2nd. It is a Saturday. If you still wish to leave that is the time. Ursula will be waiting for you. They will help you and the children find your way to a new and easier life. There will be schools for the children. Some of this money is from Clyde too. Accept it in the love it was given to you."

Finding myself now with the most difficult decision of my life to make, I knew I had to go through with it. I will pray like I have never prayed before that God will see me through this. I owe it to my children, that is what a mother does. She gives life her all. She will sacrifice all for her children.

"Thank you my dear friend. I cannot say that enough. How do I begin? I can't seem to think clearly. Suddenly my heart and mind seem all twisted ready to break at any moment."

"First of all, write something on this paper for Ursula so she will know of your intentions. I will mail it next week when we go to town. Marvin will not tell. I will find out for you when you will arrive and add that to your letter. You must stay strong. Know that Marvin and I are here for your support. We will visit you too. "

As I handed the paper back to my dear friend, I knew that now there would be no turning back. I had been saying that I needed to do this. Now the opportunity was here. I will continue with my dream for them. Bertha reminded me how these few weeks will pass so quickly. When they come to visit she will bring me a short note from Ursula that she herself has actually written. It will invite me to visit for a few weeks. Her and Marvin will be there to support what I say.

Each day when I was in the house alone, I went through my clothes and those for the children making them ready to pack. I will need to make it seem that I am just going over the box of items Ursula had sent earlier. My mind was so full that it seemed as though my thoughts were flying right out of me at lightening speed.

Next week the Faust family came to visit. She gave me her letter. With my heart pounding fiercely she told Floyd the story of how she had picked up the letter when she was inquiring of a letter from her sister. Knowing they were going to visit us she offered to take mine too. Being busy, the clerk did not give it a thought as he handed it to her knowing we were close friends. A neighbour helping a neighbour. Everyone was accustomed to seeing our families together in town and church.

As I had written my story in my mind and read it over and over, I said how much fun that would be. I even added in a part that told of how Clyde had urged me to do this when he was visiting us. Just speaking of how much I have missed Ursula brought tears to my eyes. They were not just for effect, they came from my heart.

Much to my surprise Floyd said that he thought we should go providing we would be home for Christmas. With the guiltiest heart I have ever had, I promised we would be back in time. We all agreed that none of the children should know until the day before leaving. They will not be able to contain themselves. Marvin assured him they would visit him. Bertha promised fresh bread and buns. This time my mouth did not drool.

On our next trip to town, I purchased a one-way ticket with the money from my dear siblings for the children and myself. The clerk asked me if I was going somewhere. Now what ever did he think I was going to do with the tickets. I calmly said yes, visiting my sister and quickly left.

When I stepped outside into the cold fresh air, I felt my heart rate slow down a little, just a little. It was as if I now could breathe a little easier. I knew I was not on easy street yet.

When I entered the store where I had spent so much time visiting, Mr. Bosch immediately asked if I was alright. After assuring me we were alone, I briefly told him I had just purchased three train tickets for December 2nd. While I am so excited my stomach was feeling a little sick. I told Mr. Bosch how this was the only thing I had not been truthful to my husband with. I am afraid the guilt may be too much. In his kind and gentle way he assured me that I was doing what I felt was the best for my children. If you confess or turn back now, there will not be peace in your heart.

At his suggestion, I spent some time browsing throughout his store to regain my composure. By the time I said my casual goodbye that was hiding a huge secret, I once again felt I was now back in control. I wanted the last time with my dear friend that I had relied on so often, to be a happy one.

A couple evenings later after reading the Bible, Floyd asked me if I had purchased the tickets. I felt it best to make this conversation short and simple. Then I went on to relay the idle conversation I had had with some ladies from the next community.

When Friday December 1st came, I quickly spent my alone time during the day packing my trunk. One trunk for three of us. I knew that after supper I would need to tell the children. For now I needed to finish the bread baking and other chores. My hope was that fresh bread would soften this departure for everyone. In the morning before leaving for town I would need to milk the cows, feed the chickens and make bread and butter sandwiches for our train ride. I would fill a couple Mason jars with fresh well water. That was all I had to take with us for this two-night train ride.

After supper when Floyd had returned to the barn to finish his evening chores, I told the children how we would be going to visit my sister for a couple weeks. We would be going on the train. Not understanding the impact this holiday would have on their lives, they were so very excited and eager to leave.

My next big hurdle would be to tell Floyd before retiring for the night, that I was going to take their bicycles along. I was certain this would draw suspicious questioning. I was right.

"Why do you need to take their bicycles?" he asked in an unhappy tone.

"Because they need to have something to play with in the city. They can ride them on the sidewalk."

While he settled for this answer, I did not feel that he was happy with it. Not being able to find fault with it, he let it go.

When morning finally came, the children were eager to rise. It was December 2nd. There was no urging them to get their chores done. At the last minute I decided to put a couple jars of canned sausage and one of Griebenschmalz for their bread in the sack. I wrapped them in amongst an old sweater to prevent them from breaking. I put in a fork and a knife. We would need to share. We would drink from the jars.

When we climbed into the sleigh, I found myself taking a lingering look at our little log house. For the first time I noticed how the roof was beginning to sag. There were icicles hanging from the edges. The willow trees next to the house seemed to be standing lifeless. The silver birch trees looked so barren with their branches being void of any sign of leaves or new growth. I could see the fields of white that had once been covered in golden stalks of wheat and oats. Beyond the field sat the Little School House, empty and alone. While doing my morning chores I said goodbye to Bossy and Misty. Even old Big Red just stared at me.

As we turned onto the road that would take us to Weesp, I found the home that couldn't be my forever home fade away into the snow covered trees. I watched as our little log house faded away feeling a little sad at leaving my husband behind with so many memories. Both good and bad.

As we travelled the familiar road to town, I listened to the steady clomp-clomp of the horses on the hard pack snowy road. Sometimes the runners would squeak as they slid over the dry snow. I wasn't sure that this was a sound I would miss or not.

As we travelled along, I took particular note of our neighbour's farms. I wanted this memory to be imprinted in my mind forever. Their kindness will always be with me. Even the muskeg didn't look so bad covered in white snow surrounded by a dilapidated split log fence.

Soon we were on South Road following the train tracks into town. We just pulled up to the turn-about when the Faust family came along in their shiny red sleigh. They had come to see us off. The train was already there giving the crew time to prepare to leave.

Now the time had come. Our heavy trunk was filled with all my worldly possessions. Once I began to pack I told the children not to open the lid because I didn't want them to mess it up and waste space. The truth was I had a few things from my mother that I just could not leave behind. I had carefully wrapped a pink fruit bowl with six matching serving dishes in amongst our sweaters. These I had kept packed in a box hidden in our closet that I now dream of putting them where I can see them and use them. I packed my mother's cookbook between Katrin's clothes. Between Fritz's clothes I packed my mother's pickle fork and some pictures. These were my most valued treasures.

Marvin helped Floyd load the children's bicycles and the heavy trunk onto the platform for the man with the black hat to stow away until our arrival. Now came the time for goodbyes. As Bertha hugged each of my children she pressed a book into their hands. Just something to read she said. Marvin just gave us each a quick hug saying "travel safe. See you soon." Then he turned and slowly walked a little further away leaving space for Floyd.

Now it was time for Floyd to hug his children. As they hugged each other he told them over and over how much they meant to him and that he loved them. He was rewarded with many hugs and kisses. Now it was my turn. I have never felt so much guilt in all my life. I knew I would be telling my husband another lie when he asks me if we are coming back. When I tell him I love him, I do mean it. I just can't tell him once more that I can no longer live in the North. He does not seem to understand. I know he is frightened of a move. We both still remember how difficult the move to the North was.

The conductor wearing his black hat, white shirt and tie shouts "All aboard, All aboard."

We must now get on. Fritz and Katrin have already found the perfect seat by the window where they sat waving wildly to their dad. The big smiles evident of their excitement. I needed to hurry on, he told me.

The engineer, wearing his blue striped cap and matching overalls with a red bandana tied firmly around his neck, was now blowing the horn alerting everyone that he was ready to leave town. As I listened to the sound of the whistle I felt my heart race. This was different than the whistle I had heard before that did not carry my children and I. This one was special.

As we all three looked out the window, I saw the town of Weesp move further and further into the distance until it was no longer in sight. Just a picture in my mind that I shall never forget. As I watch the north slowly begin to fade I am reminded that there is a new beginning.

Acknowledgements

I would like to thank my husband Bob for his many hours of hard work as he helped me with my limited computer skills that made this possible. His contribution of ideas helped to make me sound like my mother.

I would also like to thank my family and friends that have been so supportive as I worked to fulfill a dream I have had for many years. They pushed me forward each time I doubted myself.

While my brother is resting in heaven, I thank him for the many years he stood by me as we travelled a tough path together. He helped to get us into mischief but helped with the consequences sometimes leaving me to fend for myself.

This story of my mother is true with added fiction for interest purposes.

Other Books by Doreen Brust Johnson

Walking Barefoot in my Shoes

Sounds in my Shadow

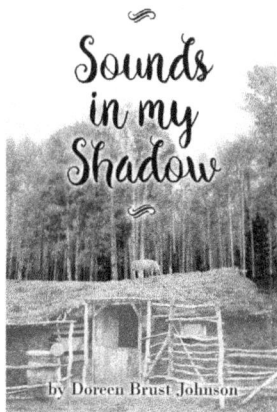

Rivershore Books

Our Young Authors Program is designed to give authors a first step into the world of publishing. We hope to encourage young authors to continue to pursue more professional publishing options as their writing and their dreams grow.

ya.rivershorebooks.com

For authors who are ready to take the next step, we also offer professional publishing options:

www.rivershorebooks.com

www.ingramcontent.com/pod-product-compliance
Lightning Source LLC
LaVergne TN
LVHW041210080426
835508LV00011B/894